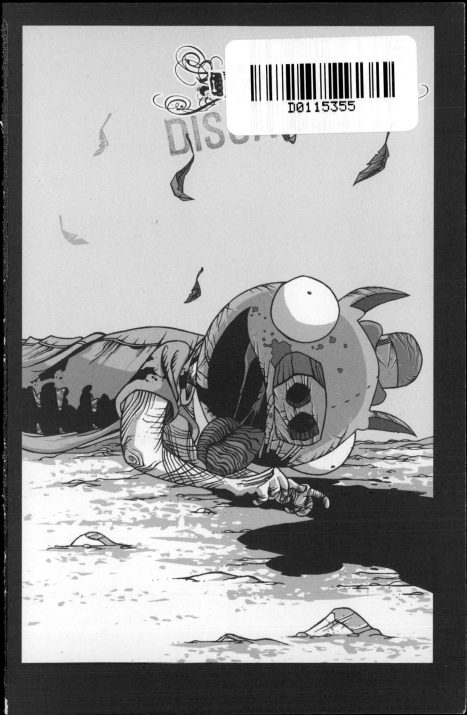

I Luv Halloween vol. 2

written by Keith Giffen

illustrated by Benjamin Roman

Lettering - James Dashiell & Jose Macasocol, Jr.
Cover Colorist - Nicolas Chapuis
Cover Design - Gary Shum
Tones - Hon Lam Chow and Studio MAKMA

Editor - Rob Valois
Digital Imaging Manager - Chris Buford
Production Manager - Jennifer Miller
Managing Editor - Lindsey Johnston
Editorial Director - Jeremy Ross
VP of Production - Ron Klamert
Publisher and E.I.C. - Mike Kiley
President and C.O.O. - John Parker
C.E.O. and Chief Creative Officer - Stuart Levy

A  Manga

TOKYOPOP Inc.
5900 Wilshire Blvd. Suite 2000
Los Angeles, CA 90036

E-mail: info@TOKYOPOP.com
Come visit us online at www.TOKYOPOP.com

ISBN: 1-59532-832-7

First TOKYOPOP printing: March 2006

10 9 8 7 6 5 4 3 2

Printed in the USA

VOLUME TWO

ART BY: BENJAMIN ROMAN
STORY BY: KEITH GIFFEN

HAMBURG // LONDON // LOS ANGELES // TOKYO

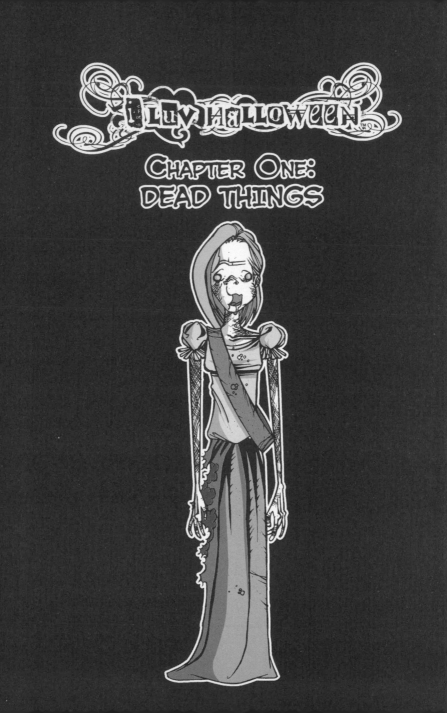

I LUV HALLOWEEN™

CHAPTER ONE: DEAD THINGS

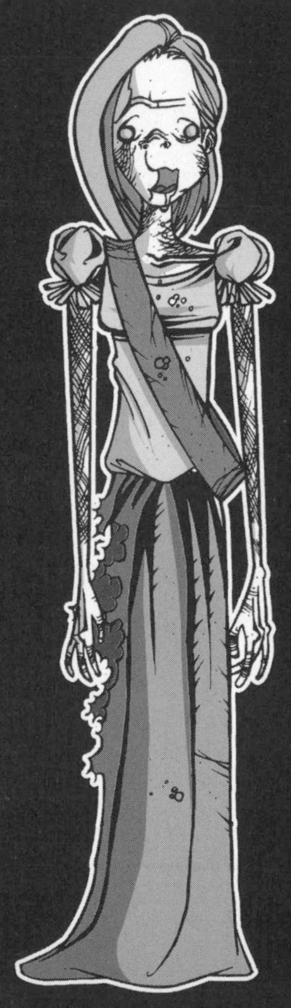

SIGH... I'M LEAVING.
ME TOO!

DO I WANT TO KNOW?
SHH! KNOWS THEY'S IN THERE... HEARS THEM ALL GIGGLY AND MAKING POO PIES FOR THE FAIR.
I DIDN'T THINK SO. YOU COMING?
LOVES THE POO PIES, THEY DOES.
FINE. STAY.
TRICKS OR TREATS! YAY!

SKREEK... CRAK!
KR-KK... THAK!
THEY HAS EATEN THE POO PIES!
SAY WHAT?

UNCLEAN! UNCLEAN!
CHOPS OUT THE CHONKLIT MONKEYS! OUT! OUT, CHONLIKT MONKEYS!
CHOKKA CHOKKA-CHOKKA-CHOKKA-CHOKKA...
PLAY NICE.
OUT! OUT! IS THE POWER OF CHRIST COMPELS YOU!
CHOKKA CHOKKA-CHOKKA-CHOKKA-CHOKKA...
CHOKKA-CHOKKA-CHOKKACHOK-KACHOKKA...
UNCLEAN! UN-CLEAN!

GL-
GNNGL..

GODDAMMIT...
IDIOT.

YOU IT?
PIG PIG GOT CHOMPED.
FOR SERIOUS? HOW'D HE MANAGE THAT? 'S NOT LIKE THEY GOT ANY MOVES OR...
EVEN NUMBNUTS HERE CAN GET AROUND THEM!
I BE SPIKE.
HE GOT CHOMPED. END OF STORY. WE DOING THIS?

THEY GET MOOCHIE TOO?
WISHFUL THINKING?
HELL YEAH!
WE DOING THIS?
SCARED MOMENT!
SHUT UP, YOU!
THOP!

YES! LET THE REVELS BEGIN!
I BE SPIKE!
HOW DID THIS HAPPEN?
HE THREATENED TO TELL.
WELL D'UH!
PARENTS ALL WEIRDED OUT BY THE WHOLE ZOMBIE THING?
WHAT? YOURS JUST LET THE TWO OF YOU GO?
REALLY? LUCKY STIFF!
KINDA.

FIGURE WE'RE THE ONLY KIDS OUT?
ISN'T THAT SARAH?
FIGURE WE'RE THE ONLY *LIVING* KIDS OUT?
MORE FOR US.
BING BONG
AMEN TO THAT!
MOOCHIE GOING OUT AS THAT TOOTH FAIRY THING AGAIN?
DO YOU CARE?
BETWEEN HER AND THAT MESSED UP *DOG* OF YOURS...
'S MOOCHIE'S DOG.

TRICK OR...

BLGRGNLCHT...

I BE SPIKE.

CLAP! CLAP!
I KNEW IT.
SEE ANYTHING LOOKS LIKE A CANDY BOWL?
THIS DOES NOT BODE WELL.
COULD BE WORSE. HE COULDA GIVEN US AN APPLE.
DO ZOMBIES DO HALLOWEEN?
SNAKT!
SNAKT!

WELL... **SURE**. I GUESS. THEY ARE MONSTERS. IT'S THEIR HOLIDAY.
NO BITE! NO BITE SPIKE! **BAD** ZOMBIE!
CHAK! KRAK! CHOKT!
WE'LL SEE.
STARTING TO WORRY ME, MAN.
I GUESS WE'LL KNOW IT'S OKAY IF **HE** SHOWS UP.
HE ALWAYS SHOWS UP.
THERE'S ALWAYS BEEN A REASON TO.
RIGHT...
SUNDAY DRIVER

MUSH

FINE THANKS. AND YOU?
Y' WELCOMES.

UH OH..
DO NOT!
DO TOO! YOU GOT THE HOT SWEETIES FOR HIM AND WANT TO MAKE KISSY FACE ALL NIGHT LONG AND HAVE HIS BABY.
DO NOT!
UH HUH!
NUH UH!
YOU TAKE THAT BACK OR I'LL--
VIVIAN AND FI-INCH SITTIN' IN A TREE...
YEAH, WELL I SEEN YOU MAKING THE OOKIEBOO EYES AT GULLY.
GET OUT! HE'S LIKE, ALL 'LEPTICAL 'N' LIKE!
YEAH? WELL AT LEAST I'M NOT ALL--
EPILEPTIC! "LEPTI-CAL"...THINK YOU COULD BE LIKE, MORE IGNORANT?

HOW LONG SHE BEEN HERE?
BEATS ME.
YOU SEE HER HOOK UP, VINNIE?
GLARGL-KKK.
EUW! COVER YOUR MOUTH! LIKE, MANNERS?!
HOW MUCH YOU FIGURE SHE HEARD?
HOW MUCH DID YOU HEAR?
JESUS! IS THAT A KNIFE?
SHE'S GOT A KNIFE?
HEY! HOW MANY TIMES YOU GOTTA BE TOLD TO COVER YOUR MOUTH?!
GLKT-MFN...
AWW, MAN! THERE'S ALL, LIKE, CRAP 'N' STUFF ON IT.

AS IF AND WHO CARES?
I THINK SHE'S, LIKE, A RETARD OR SOME-THING.
GEEZ, VERA! SHE'S ONLY STANDING RIGHT THERE.
GR-ROSS! WHAT IF SHE, LIKE, HAS TO BE FLOWER GIRL AT YOUR WEDDING?
SHU' UP! BIG EARS, RIGHT HERE.
SO?
SO YOU'RE GONNA HURT HER FEELINGS.
LOOKING TO SCORE POINTS WITH FINCHIEPOO BY COZYING UP TO HIS RETARD SISTER?
YOU LOOKING TO ADD A BLACK EYE TO THAT COSTUME?
AS IF!
UH HUH!
NUH UH!

CHOKKACHOKKA-
CHOKKACHOKKA-
CHOKKA...

!!

IS THE POWER OF CHRIST COMPELS YOU!

BING BONG

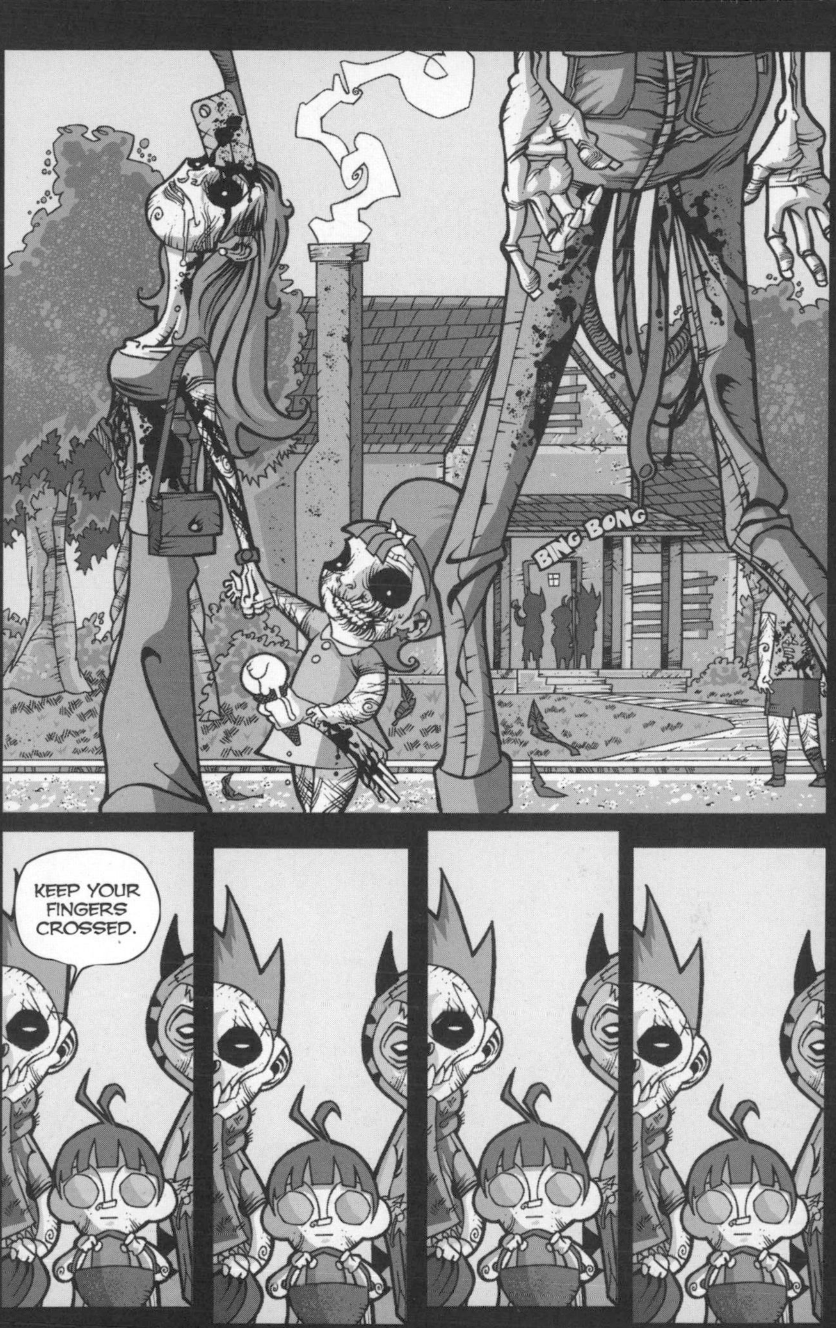

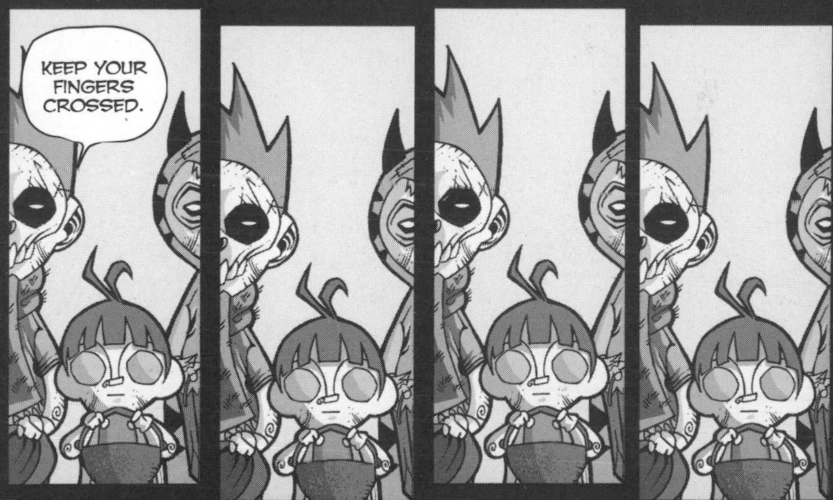
KEEP YOUR FINGERS CROSSED.

BING BONG BING
BONGBINGBONGBING
BONGBINGBONG

THIS SUCKS. BIG TIME SUCKS.

...HEARD VOICES!
SHH!
I KNOW I HEARD ...
SHUT YOUR YAP, WOMAN! AIN'T A ONE OF THEM CAN SAY DAMN ALL!

TRICK OR TREAT!

CHRISTA'MIGHTY!
CLEO! GRAB TH' OTHER ONE!

THUDDA!
THUDDA-BUMP! THUD!
HAMMER!
HAMMER-HAMMER! POUND! THUNK! THUD!
HAMMER-
HAMMER-
HAMMER!
HAMMER-

I BE SPIKE.

I Luv Halloween™

Chapter Two: Nose Candy

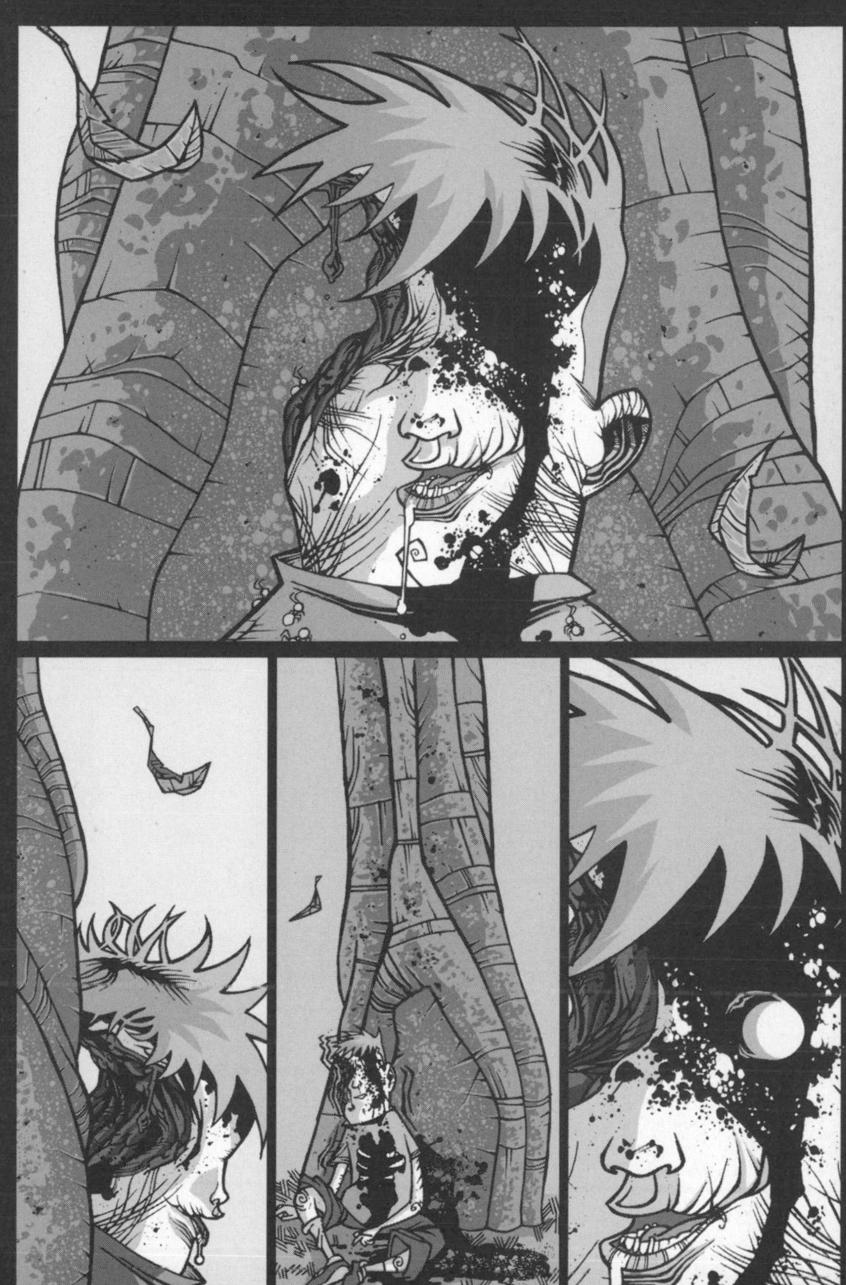

NMGHMMN...
HK!
GLK...

HUFFAPUFF...
HUFFAPUFF...
HUFFAPUFF...
HUFFAPUFF...
GASP...
HUFFA...
GASP...
PUFFA... GASP... HUFF...WHAT WAS THAT?! WHAT WAS THAT?!
AH... GEEZ! LOOK AT HER!
TOL'JA! TOL'JA SHE WAS A RETARD! NOW LOOK WHAT SHE DONE! JEEZUM CROW!
YOU SEE HER?
LOST HER.

WHATTA WE DO NOW? MOM'S GONNA KILL US!
WE DIDN'T DO NOTHING!
THAT'S EXACTLY WHAT SHE'S GONNA SAY! "SHE WAS CUTTIN' UP ON YOUR SISTER AND YOU DID NOTHING?!" WE ARE SO SCREWED!
VINNIE? IT HURT MUCH? VINNIE?
CHAWMP!
YEEEEEE!
SCREEECH!
VEWA! GED 'ER OFF! GED 'ER OFFA ME!
RAWNCH... RAWNCH... RAWNCH...
RAWNCH... RAWNCH...
YEEEEEE!
VINNIE! NO!
YEEEEEE!

CHR-RRP!
SCREEEECH!!

OMIGOD! OMIGOD! OMIGOD!
GEDDID! GEDDID BAGK!

MY NODE! MAGKE HER SPIDDIDOUD!
GET?
WHAT?!

GL-ULP
MY NODE!
YOU MAKE HER SPIT IT OUT.

GREAD... NOW WE GODDA I'DUCE VOMIDING.
INDUCE...
NO WAY!
UH HUH!
SHE ADE MY NODE!
WELL... YEAH.
HEY! WHERE YOU GOING?

YOU SEE DIS?
EUW! EUW!
GODDA GED... SUMPIN'...I DUNNO. WAID HERE TIL I GED BACK.
WITH HER?!
WAID HERE!
GRGL... GLK..
SIGH...

...LIVING DEAD! JUST LIKE IN THE MOVIES!
MOVIES. RIGHT.
SAYS SO RIGHT THERE IN THE GOOD BOOK.
REVELATIONS. SAYS SO RIGHT THERE IN BLACK AND WHITE.
BLACK AND WHITE. RIGHT.
WE BEEN LEFT BEHIND BECAUSE WE'RE SINNERS.
BIBLE
RAPTURE DONE COME AND TOOK UP THE FAITHFUL AND LEFT US TO... TO *THIS!*
RAPTURE. RIGHT.

'S ALL HERE. RIGHT HERE IN THE GOOD BOOK.
GOOD TO KNOW.
HOLY Bible
CAN WE GO NOW?
GO? OUT THERE? WITH THEM?
LOOK LADY, I'M SURE YOU THINK YOU'RE DOING THE RIGHT THING BUT--
PRAY WITH ME, BOYS.
BEER
BEER

LORD...WE DON'T KNOW WHY YOU SAW FIT TO LEAVE US BEHIND WHEN YOU TOOK THE FAITHFUL UP TO HEAVEN TO BE WITH YOU, BUT WE BOW TO YOUR ALMIGHTY WILL EVEN IF IT SEEMS A MITE UNFAIR THAT GLORIA FROM NEXT DOOR GOT TOOK, HER BEING A ***SLUT*** AND ALL AND IT AIN'T JUST ME SAYIN' SO...

ELAINE FROM DOWN THE BLOCK SEEN HER HORIZONTAL BOPPIN' THE FEDEX GUY JUST LAST WEEK. SOME FOLKS JUST DON'T GOT THE COMMON SENSE TO PULL A SHADE.
... WHERE WAS I?
HANG ON, BOYS...GOT TO REFRESH M' MEMORY.
UKUKUKUKU KUKUK...

WHY, GOD?! ***WHY?!***

SOB!
SOB-OB SOB!
CAN THIS POSSIBLY GET ANY WORSE?
SOB-OB! SOB!
I MADE S'MORES!
MACK
WHY?!
HADDA ASK...

!!
HLGHSHHGLK...
SKLGK!
YEEK!

COME 'N' GO
24-7
HNK... UGH... UF...
LOOTING?
HUH? NO! I... IT WAS...I WASN'T...
RELAX. I'M IMPRESSED. ENTREPRE-NEURIAL SPIRIT AND ALL THAT.
HUH?
IT'S A COMPLI-MENT. TRUST ME.
NEED A HAND WITH THAT?
THERE'S MORE INSIDE.
MAYBE LATER.
YOU'RE THAT KID'S ALWAYS TRICK'R TREATING WITH FINCH.
SEEN HIM?
FINCH? NO.
MISTER KITTY? PIG PIG?

WE...DON'T HANG. Y'KNOW?
YOU GOT A NAME?
GULLY.
GULLY? HULLY GULLY? THE EPILEPTIC KID?
I... GOTTA BE GOING.
FINCH SAYS YOU GOT THE MOVES.
SAYS WHEN YOU GO OFF YOU *REALLY* GO OFF.
I REALLY GOTTA GO.
THAT TRUE?
TRUE?
YOU GOT THE MOVES?
HNGH... UK... UMPH...

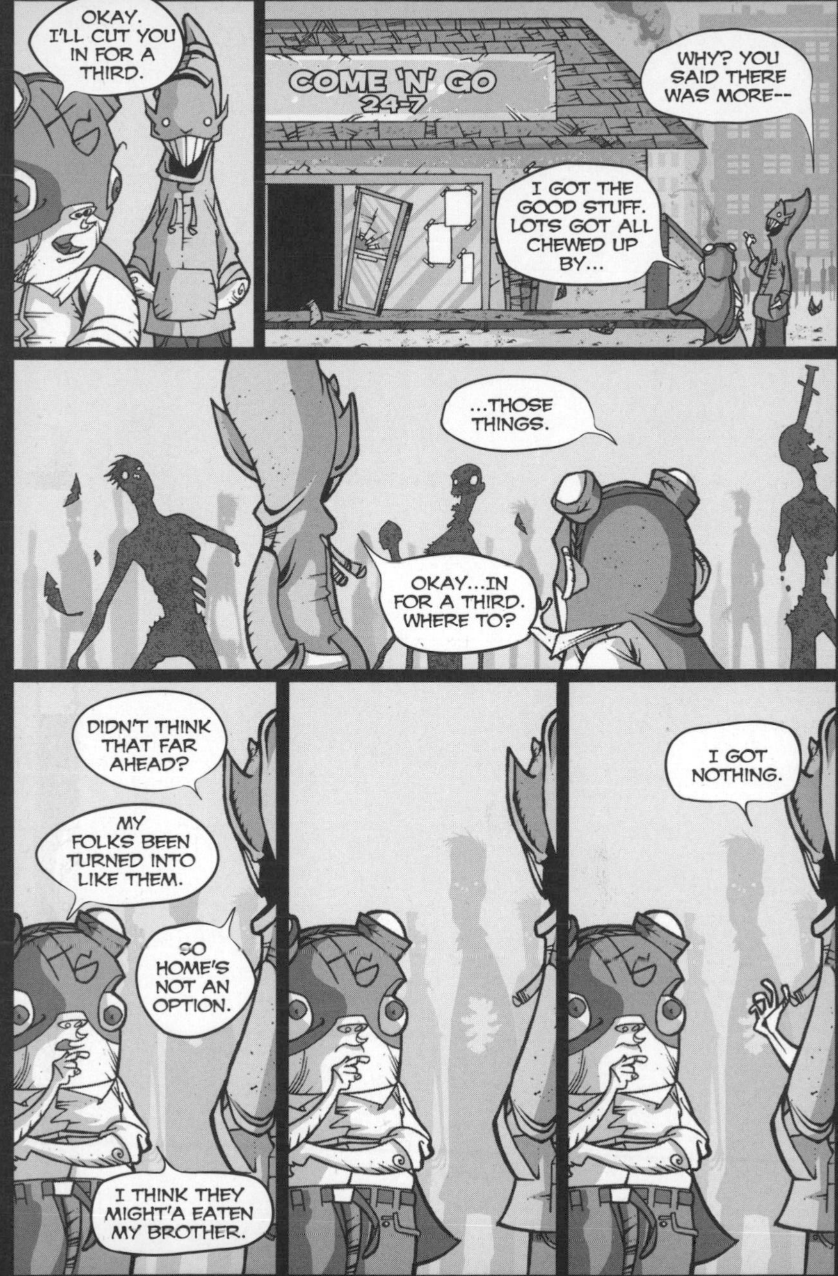
OKAY. I'LL CUT YOU IN FOR A THIRD.
COME 'N' GO 24-7
WHY? YOU SAID THERE WAS MORE--
I GOT THE GOOD STUFF. LOTS GOT ALL CHEWED UP BY...
...THOSE THINGS.
OKAY...IN FOR A THIRD. WHERE TO?
DIDN'T THINK THAT FAR AHEAD?
MY FOLKS BEEN TURNED INTO LIKE THEM.
SO HOME'S NOT AN OPTION.
I THINK THEY MIGHT'A EATEN MY BROTHER.
I GOT NOTHING.

WHAT ABOUT WE STASH IT AT YOUR HOUSE?
THAT'S NEVER A GOOD IDEA.
C'MON. WE'LL... UNGH...PLAY IT BY EAR.
SUNNU-VA...HOW MUCH... UGH...DID YOU...HF... CRAM IN HERE?
IT WAS... UK...FREE. DO THE...UNGH... MATH.
CRASH!
YEEEEK!
THUD!
B-DUMP!

?!
!!
SUNNUBA-BIDCHT!
P-TUNK!
BIDE MY EAW OFF! TEACH YOU D' BIDE PEEPL'S EAWS OFF!
CHAK! CHAK! CHAKT!
CHAK! CHAK!
WHAD? SEE SUM'PIN INDERESDIN'?
GORRY! WHAT HAPPENED TO HER NOSE?
WHAT NOSE?

DID YOU JUST SAY "GORRY"?
MY ***NODE!***
HEY! DON' YOU GO MAGIN' FUNNA MY NODE! KICK YER ASS YOU GO MAGIN'...
BWAAAAAHHHHH!
NOW SEE WHAT YOU DONE?
BWAHHHWWWWWW!
SHE'S REALLY UPSET.
D'UH!
I THINK SHE'S MISSING AN ***EAR*** TOO.
MY ***EAW!*** BWAAAHHHH!

BWAHHHHH!

B-B-B-B-G-G-G-G-G...

...WONDERFUL.

I GOTTA, MACK! I GOTTA!
NO, DARLIN'. NO YOU DON'T.
YOU TYIN' ONE ON AIN'T GONNA DO NO ONE NO GOOD 'CEPT THEM THINGS OUTSIDE.
THEM THINGS OUTSIDE USED T' BE OUR FRIENDS 'N' NEIGHBORS! HOW'D THIS HAPPEN, MACK? HOW'D WE GET LEFT BEHIND?
LORD WORKS IN MYSTERIOUS WAYS...
WOULDN'T GIVE US ONE OF OUR OWN 'N' NOW THIS. AIN'T FAIR, MACK. AIN'T FAIR AT ALL!
WE COULDN'T HAVE KIDS OF OUR OWN.
DO TELL.
CAN WE GO NOW?
DOCTORS CALLED IT AN OCCLUDED UTERUS. MACK'S LI'L SWIMMERS COULDN'T PUNCH THROUGH.
CAN WE SEE?

THWOK!
HEY... OW!
JUST FIGURED IF WE'RE GONNA BE STUCK HERE, MIGHT AS WELL GET SOME-THING OUT OF IT.
I GOTTA GO.
NUMBER ONE OR NUMBER TWO?
DOWN TH' HALL. FIRST DOOR ON YOUR RIGHT.
I REALLY GOTTA...
MACK
EER
EER

BEST GO WITH HIM, MACK. IN CASE ONE'A THEM THINGS BREAKS IN WHILE HE'S ON THE POTTY.
I'LL JUST...WAIT OUT HERE, IT'S ALL TH' SAME T' YOU.
THERE IS A GOD.

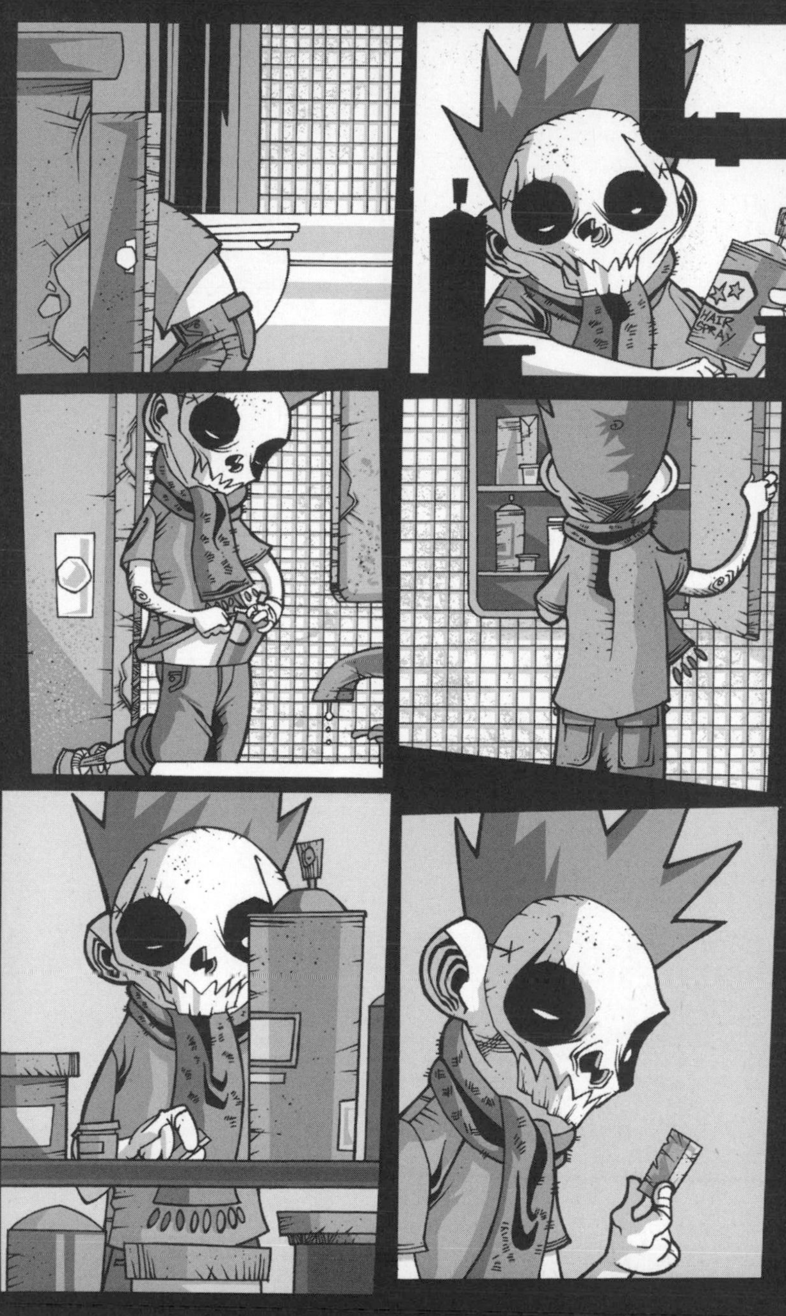
HAIR SPRAY

ALL SET?
FLUSH-SH
HOW LONG ARE YOU PLANNING ON KEEPING US HERE?
LONG'S IT TAKES, SON, SO DON'T YOU WORRY.
FEELING BETTER, HON'?
A MITE. THE BOY OKAY?
'BOUT'S WELL'S CAN BE EXPECTED. ALL THINGS CONSIDERED...
IT WAS GOD'S WILL WE FOUND THEM.
HE'S OFFERED US UP A CHANCE FOR SALVATION.
SURE, HON'. SURE.
WELL SURE HE HAS.

GIVE US THE CHANCE T' PROVE OURSELVES WORTHY OF HIS DIVINE GRACE.
WHAT?
YOU'RE KIDDING.
SHE SHOWED YOU?
OH YEAH.
SURE DID.
AND?
AND WHAT?
YOU'RE NOT GONNA GET ALL WEIRD ABOUT HER, ARE YOU?
HELL NO! SHE'S ALL OCCLUDED UP IN THERE.
GOOD. THEN I CAN COUNT ON YOU TO DO WHAT NEEDS DOING?
DEPENDS.
YOU WANT TO SPEND THE REST OF THE NIGHT IN HERE WITH THEM?
GO ON.
WE'RE GONNA HAVE TO KILL THEM.

I Luv Halloween

Chapter Three: CHONKLIT MONKEYS

TOY STORE
K-KICK ASS... K-KICK ASS... K-KICK ASS...
K-KICK ASS K-KICK ASS... K-KICK ASS...
AISLE ONE 
AISLE TWO
IS THE *POO-POCALYPSE!*
TOY BIN
DOLLS
SEES THEM OUT THERE, WE DOES. THEY HAS EATEN THE ***POO PIES*** AND GROWED ***CHONKLIT MONKEYS*** UP IN THE POOTY PARTS.
THEY HAS BEEN ***POOSSESSED***.

HEARS THEM DOWN THE IN POO PIPES, CHONKLIT MONKEYS ALL GIGGLY AND SINGING THEY DURAN DURAN AND BAKING POO PIES FOR THE FAIR.
THINKS THEY'S MAKING THE *BIG SECRETS*, THEY DOES!
BUT WE KNOWS...

HEARS THEM DOWN THERE PAST THE *POOTY SEAT*. KNOWS THEM. YES WE DOES.

UNCLEAN! CUTS THEM OUT OF THE POOTY PARTS AND SPANKS THEY BROWN BOTTOMS! SENDS THEM BACK TO THE POO PLACE! YES!

POOT!

UNCLEAN!!

UNCLEAN! UNCLEAN! YEEEEEEE!
HG

SOU'DED LIGE FINTZ'S SISDER. TH' *CRAZY* 'UN?
I DON'T WANT TO KNOW.
YOU KNOW FINCH?
I SEED 'IM AROUD. AIN' SEED 'IM T'NIGHD.
CAWFUH! ID BUWNS LIGE A SUNUBBA DITCH.
THIS GONNA TAKE MUCH LONGER?
FUH *GOO,* GUHEE.
NAH. I'M DONE. YOU WANT A LOOK?
NUH UH!
HEY! AIN' JOO GON' PUD ON A *BANNIDGE* 'R' SUMIN'?
HELL NO. I WAS JUST TAKING IN THE VIEW. *WAY* GROSS!

ODAY... ODAY... THAD TH' WAY ID'S GONNA BE! FI'. JUDS *FI'!* GED MY ***OWO*** BANNIDGE.

MEBBE EBEN FI' A ***NEW*** NODE T' SEW ON! YEAH! LIGE A DRANDP-LAND.

SO ***LIFT*** AL-READY!

I ***AM!***

I DON'T WANT TO BE AT THIS ALL NIGHT.

I AM!

DID YOU SAY TRANSPLANT?
FUH GOO!
AS IN, STICK ON A NEW NOSE?
I DON'T THINK YOU'RE GONNA FIND ANY SPARE NOSES IN THERE.
C'MON, MAN!
FUH GOO!
FUH GOO!
GOT NOSES TO SPARE OUT HERE. EARS TOO.
WHUH?

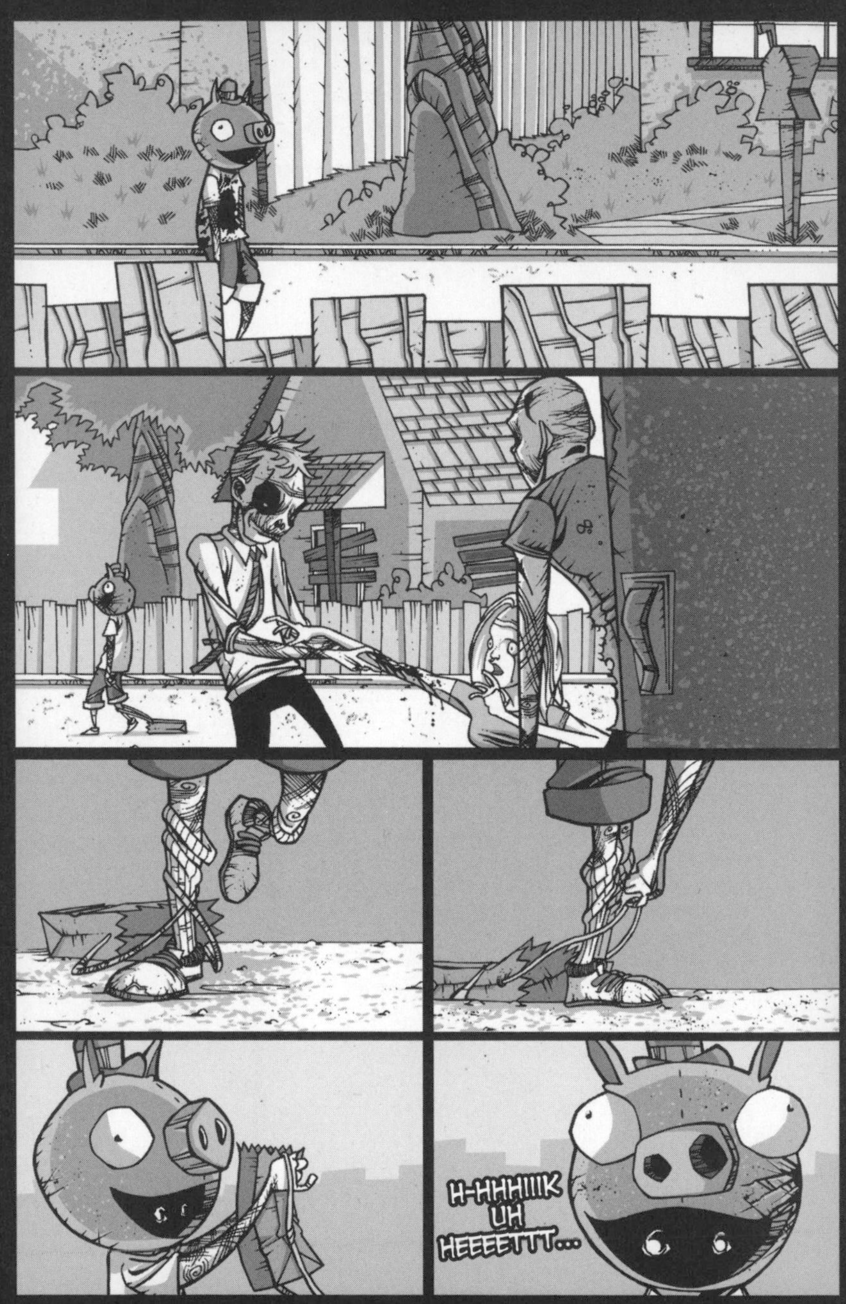
H-HHHIIIK
UH
HEEEETTT...

BING
BONG
BING
BONG
BING
BONG
BING
BONG

HHHI-IIK
UH
HEEEET-TT...

H-HHHIIIK UH
HEEEET-TT...
H-HHHI-IIK UH
HEEEET-TT...
HHIIIK UH
HEEET-
EETT...
HHHHIKUH...
HEEEET...

NO!
VINCENT! STAY!
VINCENT, NO! NO!
BAD, VINCENT! BAD! NO SQUIRRELS! BAD, VINCENT!
GIMME THAT! SPIT!
SPIT IT OUT OR I TELL MOM!
SPIT! SPIT! YOU'RE GONNA HAVE SQUIRREL BREATH!
STOP CHEW-ING!
EUW! EUW! IT'S MAKING CRUNCHIES! IT'S--
POP!

YEEEEEEE!
PIG PIG?

...ACTING ALL GROSS LIKE AND EUW AND SHE'S REALLY BEGINNING TO WEIRD ME *OUT*, Y'KNOW?
JUST UP HERE. *C'MON ALREADY!*
'S NOT LIKE WE'RE GONNA *MAKE OUT* OR LIKE.
'S JUST SHE'S ACTING ALL CRAZY LIKE AND YOU GOTTA STAY WITH ME TIL VIVIAN GETS BACK 'CAUSE SHE'S ACTING REALLY, *REALLY* CREEPY.
SO YOU'LL, LIKE, HANG TIL VIV GETS BACK, RIGHT?
RIGHT?
PIG PIG?

UNCLEAN! UNCLEAN! OUT, CHONKLIT MONKEYS!
FEELS THE BURN!
SPLISH! SPLISH! SPLISH!
OUT! OUT, CHONKLIT MONKEYS! IS THE POWER OF CHRIST COMPELS YOU!
I FEELS THE SPIRIT IN ME! YAY!
CLEANS THE POO PARTS! HOLY FIRE! HOLY FIRE! YAY!
THID ID RIDIGALUS.

YOU HELP US STASH THE GOODS, WE HELP YOU HUNT UP... SPARE PARTS
COULD'A LEFD ID 'HIND SUM BUSHIDS 'N' COME BAG **LADER** FOR ID. THEY DON' EAD **CANDY**, THEY EAD **PEEPUL**.
AND ANIMALS. SAW OLD LADY MELCHER EATING ONE'A HER CATS.
REALLY GROSS.
I THINGK VINCEND'S TURNING INDO ONE'A DEM.
VINCENT?
MY SISDER.
YOUR SISTER'S NAME IS VINCENT?
MY PAWENDS COULD'N THINGK UF ANUDDA GUHLS NAME BEGINS WI' "V."
VANESSA, VALERIE, VIVICA, VIRGINIA, VELMA-
YEAH! **VELMA!** LIKE ON SCOOBY DOO!

FROM WHEN I WAS, LIKE, A LITTLE KID...
YEEK! YEEK! YEEEEEE...
YEEK! YEEK! YEEEEEE...
YOUR SISTER. RIGHT?
VEWA?
GORRY! ISN'T THAT THAT PIG PIG KID?
YOUR *OTHER* SISTER. RIGHT?
ARE DEY HOWDIN' HAN'S?

YIEEEEEEE!!
HHHI-IIK UH HEEEET-TT...
HH-IIIK UH HEET...
HHHIKUH... HEEEET...
ARE THEY SAYING WHAT I THINK THEY'RE SAYING?
NO! BAD, BINCEN'! SDOP! SDOP ID OR I DELL MOM!
HEY! WE'RE SUPPOSED TO BE--
HEWWO? A LIDDLE HE'P HEAH?
DID IT SOUND LIKE THEY WERE SAYING "TRICK OR TREAT"?

LIKE WHO WAS SAYING "TRICK OR TREAT"?
THE ZOM-BIES!
ZOMBIES GO TRICK OR TREATING?
NO! NO BID-ING! BIN-CEN'! NO!

SHRIEK!

MY FINGUH! BID MY FINGUH OFF! SUMMUDA-BIDCH! BID MY FINGUH OFF!
MAN...SHE DIDN'T HAVE BAD LUCK SHE'D HAVE NO LUCK AT ALL.
JEEKERS! SHE'S BLEED-ING ALL OVER!
JEEKERS?

SHE'S GONNA GET BLOOD ON EVERY-THING!
JEEKERS?!

WHA?! DID'N YOU SEE I NEE'ED HE'P? STAN' DERE 'N' WADTCH ME WEDSUWING WID DEM 'N' DON' DO NUH'IN?!
BID MY FINGUH OFF!
JEEKERS!
HUH?
NOTHING. HEAD'S UP.
HUH?!
DA DID ID, BINCEN'! I'M DELLIN' MOM YOU T'YIN' T' EAD PIHPUL!
KICK!
SHE BID MY NODE OFF.
WELL, AT EAST SHE KEPT IT IN THE FAMILY.
WHAD?
NOTHING.

PIG'S WEAWY BEGINNIN' T' ANNOY MIH.
C'MON! LET'S GET GOING!
IT'S PART OF HIS CHARM.
HEY! WHEA DO YOU T'INK YOU'W GOIN'? BINCEN'! BINCEN'!!
ZOMBIE LOVE. NOT TOO GROSS.
MAYBE SHE'LL POOP IT OUT.
POOP?
VIVIAN'S NOSE.
DO ZOMBIES POOP?
LIGE CAWN?
CORN? DID YOU SAY CORN?
YOU WEAWY THINGK BINCEN' MIGHD POOB OUD MY NODE?
IT COULD HAPPEN.

NO WAY AM I FOLLOWING A ZOMBIE AROUND WITH A POOPER SCOOPER.
REALITY CHECK. IT'S GONNA COME OUT ALL CHEWED UP 'N' DIGESTED LIKE. YOU WANT SOMETHING LIKE THAT FRONT AND CENTER ON YOUR FACE?
ID'S MY NODE!
THERE'S NO SHORTAGE OF NOSES OUT HERE.
YOU GET TO CHOOSE THE PRETTIEST...
YOU SAYIN' MY NODE WUD'N PWETTY?
SIGH...
C'MON ALREADY!

HHHIIK UH HEEEET-TT...
HH-III-KK UH HEET...
HHHHI-IIKUH... HEEET...

NO SCREAMINGS.
EEP!

VERY QUIET. SHHH. HEARS US THEY COMES AND POOSSESSES THE FOOTIE PARTS.
CHONKLIT MONKEYS...
OMIGOD...

DON'T STAB ME... DON'T STAB ME... PLEASE, OH PLEASE, DON'T STAB ME...
MAKES THE TASTY POO PIES, THEY DOES.
MAKE A PUFFY!
WH-HUH?!
MAKE A PUFFY! SMELLS YOUR BREATH FOR THE POO PIES!
PF...
SNF!
SNF-F!
SNF!
SNF!
CLEAN...
YOU'RE NOT, LIKE, GONNA DO NO RETARD STUFF TO ME...ARE YOU?

IS YOU AND ME.
HUH?
GOTS TO FIND THE KING OF THE CHONKLIT MONKEYS AND CUTS HIM OUT OF THE POOTY PARTS AND SENDS HIM BACK TO THE POO PLACE!
KING...?
SPANKS HIS BROWN BOTTOM, WE DOES! MAKES HIM TAKE HIS POO PIES BACK FOR HAPPILY EVER AFTER AND TRICK OR TREATER TIME!
...FOR REAL?

Chapter Four:
HHHIK UH HEEET

GOD IN HEAVEN! **GOD** IN HEAVEN!

I GOTCHA, HON'! I GOTCHA!

YEEEEEEEEEEEEE...MNFPH!

I KNOW IT HURTS!

MF! MF H'N B'DEE! MF!

SICK, MAN! SHE SMELLS LIKE BACON!

UPSTAIRS!

GOD IN ***HEAVEN,*** CLEO!

KILL YOU! KILL TH' BOTH'A YOU JERKWEASEL, SPUNK MONKEY SONS 'A' BITCHES!
MADE YOU S'MORES! MADE YOU S'MORES 'N' THIS IS WHAT I GET?! YOU BOYS BE DEAD!!
MF!
MF'NGN'N'D B'DEE!
SMOTHER!
BEE

HE SOUNDS AWFUL MAD.
YOU SET HIS WIFE ON FIRE.
DAMMITALL! DID HE BOARD EVERYTHING OVER?!
SKIN YOU LI'L NO 'COUNT MAGGOTS ALIVE!
I MADE YOU S'MORES, GODDAMMIT!
HE'S REALLY GOT A HARD ON ABOUT THOSE S'MORES.
IN HERE. WE CAN BARRICADE THE DOOR.
I DUNNO... HE'S AW-FUL BIG...
HELP ME GET THE DRESSER SHOVED OVER. THEN WE CAN GO TO WORK ON THOSE BOARDS.
UNK...UK... WHAT IF HE... UGH...CHASES US OUT...HK... SIDE?
WELL...D'UH! YOU...UK...SET HIS...UGH-UK...WIFE ON FIRE...UF...
NOOOOOO! DEAR GOD IN HEAVEN, NOOOOO!
YOU...HF... DON'T FIGURE HE'S, LIKE, OVER...UK... REACTING? SHE WAS DAMAGED... HF...GOODS.
OCCLUDED... HF... RIGHT?
BIG TIME... UNK....

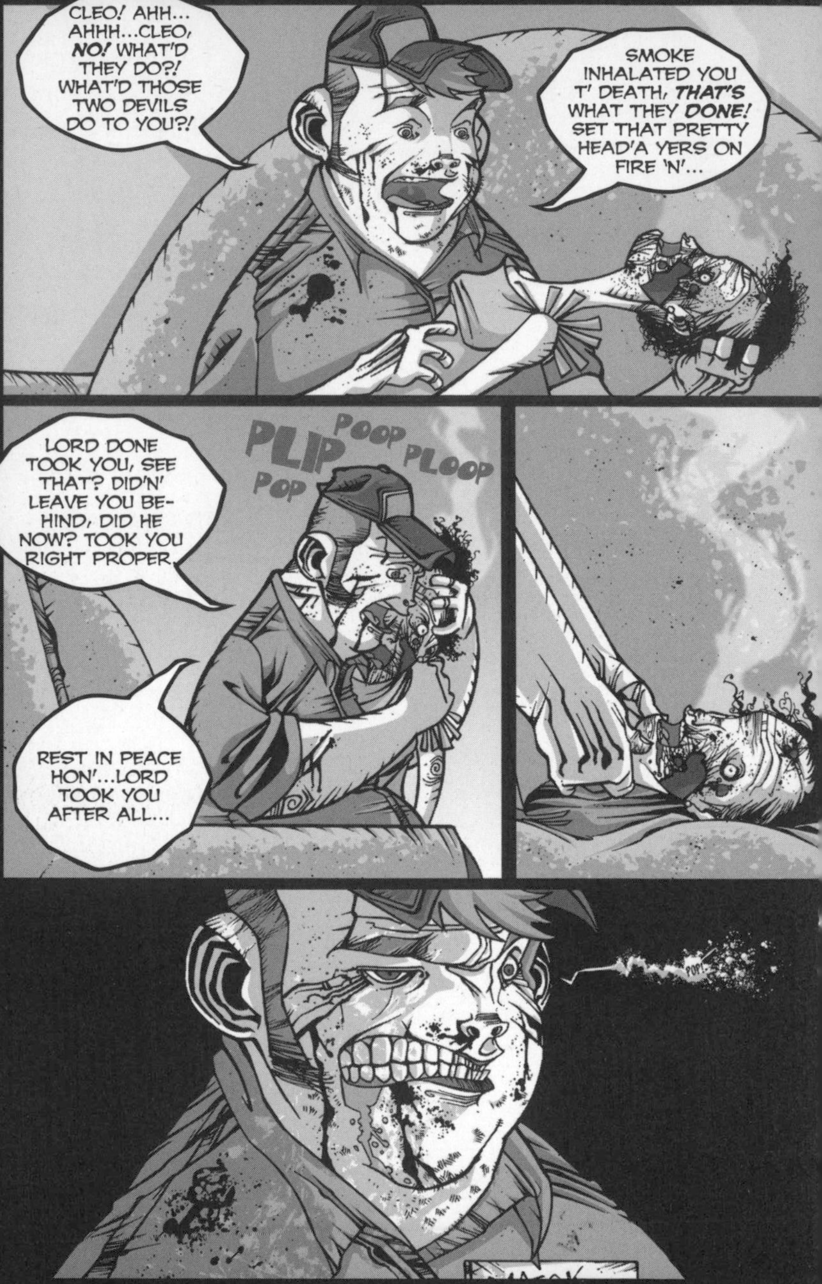

CLEO! AHH... AHHH...CLEO, ***NO!*** WHAT'D THEY DO?! WHAT'D THOSE TWO DEVILS DO TO YOU?!

SMOKE INHALATED YOU T' DEATH, ***THAT'S*** WHAT THEY ***DONE!*** SET THAT PRETTY HEAD'A YERS ON FIRE 'N'...

PLIP POOP PLOOP POP

LORD DONE TOOK YOU, SEE THAT? DID'N' LEAVE YOU BE-HIND, DID HE NOW? TOOK YOU RIGHT PROPER.

REST IN PEACE HON'...LORD TOOK YOU AFTER ALL...

HHHIIK UH HEEEET-TT...
HHHHI-IIKUH... HEEET...
HH-III-KK UH HEET...
HHIKUH HEEEE....
HI-IHHK UH HEEEK...
HHH-IIIIKUH... HEEEK...
P.B.W IS A JERK
HIIK UH HEET-TT...
IIIIK UH HEET-TT
HHI-IIK... UHEEET...
WHAT DO WE DO? THEY'RE, LIKE, EVERYWHERE!
HEARS THEM? HEARS WHAT THEY'S SAYINGS? MAKING THE TRICKINGS OR TREATINGS THEY IS! HEARS THEM?

THEY IS MAKING THE HIJACKING OF THE TRICKINGS OR TREATINGS FOR THE *CHONKLIT MONKEYS!* TAKES AWAY ALL OF THE CANDY, THEY DOES, AND FILLS THEY BAGS WITH THE POO PIES!
IS THAT WHAT THEY'RE SAYING? "TRICK OR TREAT?"
SOON... *SOON* THEY BE SINGING THEY DURAN DURAN AND MAKING THE GRABBIES!
G- GRABBIES?
IS MOST HORRIBLE OF ALL AND UNSPEAK-ABLES!
SHOULDN'T I, LIKE, HAVE A BETTER WEAPON?
IS FOR MASHING THEY POO PIES. SMACKS THE POO PIES WITH IT! SMACKS THE POO PIES BACK INTO THEY BROWN BOTTOMS! SPANKS THEY BROWN BOTTOMS WE DOES!
SCREEE-KRAK! KRAK-AK! RAWNCH!
ME? YOU NEVER SAID NOTHING 'BOUT ME DOING THE SPANKING.
FINDS THE KING OF THE CHONKLIT MONKEYS AND CUTS HIM OUT OF THE POOTY PARTS. FINDS HIM AND MAKES IT TRICK OR TREATER TIME AGAIN.

THUD!
CLUDDA-THUD!
NO...REALLY. THIS WHOLE SPANKING BROWN BOTTOMS THING? HELLO? MOOCHIE...?
THUD!
THUD!
THUD!
WHUK!
UK!
THUD! THUD!
OW...OW... CHEAP ASS WOOD!
THUD! THUD!
THUD!
SAVE IT FOR LATER.
IT HURTS NOW!
THUD! KRAK-ASH!
...KILL YOU DEADER'N DOG MEAT!!
LATER. RIGHT.

HHIKUH HEEEE...
I BE SPIKE.
HI-IHHK UH HEEEK...
HHH-IIIIKUH... HEEEK...
HHI... KUH HEEEE....
RAAARRRGH!
HI-IHHK UH-HEEEK...
MACK
BEEE... SBIIII-KG...
HHH-IIIIKUH... HEEEK...HIII BE...SBIIIKE...

OW! OW! GEDDIDOFFAMEEEEE!
THUDDA-BUMP!
THEY GOT THE CANDY!
CRASH!
KRAK-UNCH!
THWOK!
HOLD **STILL!**
OW! OW-OW-SCREEEECH!

WHACK!
OVER HERE!
CLUDDA-BUMP!
MY EYE! SUDDA-BICHIDS POGDED OUD MY *EYE!*
THEY'VE GOT THE CANDY!!
THUNK!
GET ***OVER*** IT!
CLATTER!

COME...***ON!***
THE CANDY! THE ***CANDY!!***
POGDED OUD MY EYE 'N' ***ADE*** ID!

OUR CANDY!!
SCREW THE CANDY!
SLAM!
MY EYE!
BWAHHHHHHHHHHHH!
YOUR PARENTS, RIGHT?
WHAT'D THEY WANT THE CANDY FOR? THEY EAT PEOPLE, RIGHT?
B-DUMP! BUMP!
BWAHHHHHHHHHHHHHH!
THUD!
OKAY...I'M THINKING IF WE CIRCLE AROUND AND SNEAK IN THROUGH THE KITCHEN...
SOME MORE THAN OTHERS.
BWAHHHHHHHHHHHH!
THUDDA!
WHUD!
BUMP-UMP!
WHAT *IS* IT WITH YOU AND THAT CANDY?
IT'S *MINE!!* I FOUND IT! THAT'S LIKE, SQUATTER'S RIGHTS OR SOMETHING!
H-HH... H-H-HH...
WHUD!
THUDDA!
BUMP-UMP!

ONLY IF YOU LIVE IN THE BAG.
HUH?
NEVER MIND.
SNRK... NOW I NEEDA GEDDA EYE DOO!
WHUNK! THUD! CHUD!
I DUNNO... THE LOOK WORKS FOR YOU...
YOU PROMID'D! YOU PROMID'D YOU'D HEP ME FIN' UDDAH PAHTS!
DID YOU GET IT IN WRITING?
CHOKE ON IT! CHOKE ON IT!!
BUMP! WHAP! CLUDDA-BUMP!
BWAAAAHHHHHH!
ICK...
DUDE?
WHAM! BAM! THUD!
BWAAAAHHHHHHH!
B-B-G- B-G-G- B-B-B- G-G- G...
SIGH...
SEIZURE!
THUD! B-DUMP! BUMP!

VIVIAN?
......
BAM!
SNRK... H-HH... VEWA?
BUMP!
WHACK!
G-G-B-G-B- G-G-B-B-B-G- G-G...
OMIGOD! OMIGOD, VIVIAN! YOU'RE ALL, LIKE, GROSS AND, LIKE, OMIGOD!
BWAAAHHHHHH!
G-G-B-G- B-G-G-B- B-B-G-G- G...
THUD!
BUMP!
B-BUMP!
DEY KEEBS ON EADIN' ME!
VINCENT ATE A SQUIRREL! IT WAS ALL CRUNCHING AND NOW SHE'S MAKING COOCHIE EYES AT PIG PIG!
IS THAT A SPATULA ?
BWAAAHHHHHH!
B-B-B-G- B-G-G-G- B-G-B-B...
THEY'RE, LIKE, HOLDING HANDS!
BAM! THUD! BAM!
THIS? YEAH. MOOCHIE 'N' ME, WE'RE GONNA HUNT DOWN THE ZOMBIE KING GUY AND... UH...
THE REST GETS KINDA ICKY.
MOOCHIE... YOU'RE WITH MOOCHIE...
B-G-B G-B-B- G-G-B- G-B-B...
UFF!
WHUD! BAM! THOK!

IS THE YIPPIE-KAY-HOO! RIDE 'EM COWBOYS! YAY!

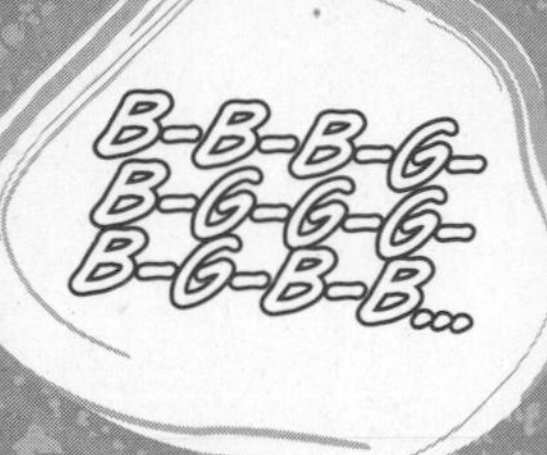
B-B-B-G-
B-G-G-G-
B-G-B-B...
WHAM!
THWAK!
BAM!
YEAH... WELL...
MADE SENSE AT THE TIME?
H-HH... SNRK... H...
SORTA...

!!
SNF SNF-NF...
B-B-B-G-B-
G-G-G-B-G-
B-B...
WHAM!
THWAK!
BAM!
SMELLS THEM! YES WE DOES! SMELLS THEM DOWN IN THEY POOTIE PLACE! IS THE CHONKLIT MONKEYS... SMELLS THEM!
THIS OUGHT TO BE GOOD.
THUD!
WHUD!
THUD!
B-B... G... G-B... UNGH...
GANGWAY!!
BAM!
?!
?
!!
THWHUD!
WHOK!
QUICK! IN HERE! WE CAN--

!!
!!
SL-LAM!
THRACK!
CRASH!
YEEEEEEE!
WHUMP!
KTASH!
WELL, SURE. WHY NOT?

RIP!
AAGGHHH!
THWOK!
GETCHA GOOD, Y' NO ACCOUNT PECKERWOOD SONS'A...

THUDDA-BUMP!
P-TOOM!
CRASH!
SHRIEK!
POK!

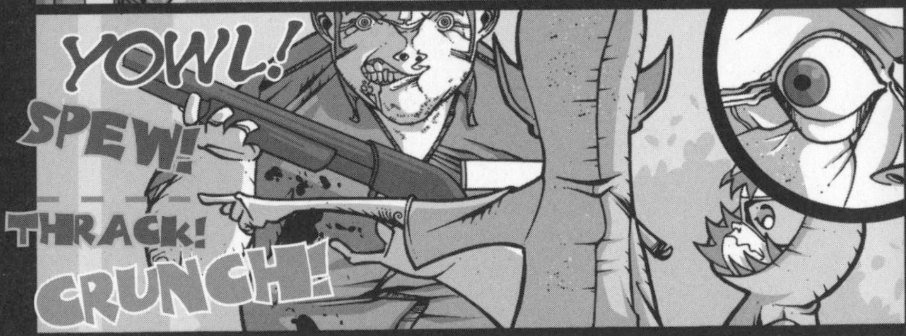
YOWL!
SPEW!
THRACK!
CRUNCH!

IS THE POOPOCA-LYPSE...
HONK!
POW!
TWEET!
SCREECH!

COMIN'A' GETCHA!
COMIN'A' GETCHA GOOD!
SMACK!
CLANG!
BEEP!
HONK!
WHUNK!
WHOOMP!

BLOW YOU BOYS RIGHT TO HELL! SEE IF'N I DON'T!!

SL-LAM!
BLAM!
BLAM!
YOU SEE THAT?! SHE WAS TRYING TO GRAB MY WEINER!
LESS TALK, MORE RUN!

WASN'T THAT, LIKE, FINCH AND THAT SPENCER KID?
UH HUH.
AIN' DEY YOWR FRENS?

RRRAARGHH!
MACK
GASP!

KILL YOU!
KILL YOU BOTH DEAD!
NOT TONIGHT.
THE CANDY!
IS THE KING OF THE CHONKLIT MONKEYS ...
YAY!

IS TO ARMS! TO ARMS! IS THE KING OF THE CHONKLIT MONKEYS!
OH GEEZ... OH GEEZ... WE GOTTA GET YOU HOME.
NUH UH! NUH UH! MOM'LL BE AWL LIGE, "WHERE'D YOU NODE" AN' "WHA'D YOU DO WID YER EYEBAW" AN' I'LL GED GROWDED.
YEEK!
HEY! DAT'S MY SISDER!
MAKES FAST AFTER HIM WE DOES! SPANKS HIS BROWN BOTTOM! YAY!
HEY!
VIVIAN!
YES! IS VIVIAN! KING OF THE CHONKLIT MONKEYS! SPANKS HIS BROWN BOTTOM, WE DOES!
WHAT?

HHI...KUH HEEEE....
HI-IHHK UHHEEEK...
BEEE...SBIIII-KG...
HHIIIIKUH HEEEK...
HIII BE SBIIIKE...
HIKUH...
HEEET...
I BHEEE...
SBIIIKE...
RRRIP!
SLUTCHA-SPLUSH!

KRUNCH!
SHHRR-RIP-PP-CHKT...

Pheebs
69
HK-ICK...

SPLUT!

P-THUD!

HHIKUH HEEEE....
HI-IHHK UHHEEEK...
BEEE...
SBIIII-KG...
HHIKUH HEEEK...
HIII BE SBIIIKE...

Chapter Five:

King of the Chonklit Monkeys

HHI...KUH HEEEE....
HIHHK UHHEEEK...
BEEE...SBIIII-KG...
HIII BE SBIIIKE...
HHIKUH HEEEK...
NO! I BE SPIKE!
BE...SBIIIGE...
HHIKUH...
HEEE...I BE...
SPIGE...
NO! BAD ZOMBIE! I BE SPIKE!
BE...
SBIIIGE...
HIK...UH-
HEET...
NO!
I BE
SPIKE!
HIKUHHH...HEEET...
BE SBIGE...
NO! I BE SPIKE!
HHIKUH
HEEEE....
HIHHK UHHEEE...
BEEE...SBIIII-KG...
HHIKUH HEEEK...
HIII BE SBIIIKE...
HIKKUH HEEEE...
BE...SBIIIGE...

BEEE...SBIIII-KG...
HHIKUH HEEEK...
HI!I BE SBIIIKE...
HIKKUH HEEEE...
BE...SBIIIGE...
HHHH...IKUHHEET...
HIKUHH...HEET...
BE SBIGE...
HIK...UH...HEEEE...
MMMACKG...
'CLUDED,
MA-AAAACK...
MMMAAAAACKG...

HF... HFFA... PF... HFFA...
HF...

GODDAMMIT!

SHE WAS **DAMAGED GOODS**, MAN! GET OVER IT!

GRRAHRRGH!

SHH...

IS THE POO PIPE!

NUH UH. **NO** WAY!

THAT'S LIKE, A SEWER OR SOMETHING. I COME BACK ALL DIRTY, MY MOM'LL PITCH A ***FIT***.

HIIK UH
HEET-TT...
HIII-KK UH
HEET...
HHI-IIK...UHEEET...
BE SBIIIGE...
HIIKUH HEET-TT...
BE SBIGE...HIII-
KK UH HEET...
WHICH
WAY?
WHAT? I'M
ALLUVA SUDDEN
A SEWER
CONNOISSEUR?
OVER HERE!
C'MON!
HHI-IIK...UHEEET...
HIIK UH HEET-TT...
HIKK UH HEET...
HHI-IIK...UHEEET...
BE SBIIIGE...
RRRAARGH!
SPANKS
HIS BROWN
BOTTOM!
YAY!
...SBIGE...HIIK
UH HEET-TT...
HIII-KK UH HEET...
HHI-II-
KUHEEET...BE
SBIIIGE...
EUW!
EUW!
EUW!
HI...IK UH
HEETT...
MMMA-
AACKG...
HIII-KK UH
HEE...EET...
HHI-IIKUHEEET...
BE
SBIIIGE...

Hardware
tools & Supplies
BAD STINKY CHEESE LADY. NO TREATS. BAD, ***BAD*** STINKY CHEESE LADY.
Restroom
...GONNA HURD?
WELL...YEAH. I MEAN, THEY'RE ***STAPLES.***
WHADDA BOUD TABE?
TAPE?
MAYBE DUCT TAPE... IF YOU'RE INTO THE WHOLE MASKED WRESTLER LOOK.
VEWY FUNNY. HOW BIG AH DOSE SDAPUHS?
SHOULD GET THE JOB DONE.

BUD ID'S GONNA HURD... RIGHD?
I'M GOING TO SAY... YES.
I BE SPIKE.
WE DOING THIS OR NOT?
OH... GREAD...ID'S SPENDZER'S IDIOD KID BRUDDA.
HELLO, ZOMBIE DINNER GIRL.
I GUESS...
YOU COMING?
THEY GLOOPED ALL OVER IT!
ALRIGHTY THEN.
ALL OF IT. THE *WHOLE BAG* ALL GOOED UP AND ZOMBIE GLOOPED. ALL THAT *CANDY*...
I MEAN, HOW FAIR IS *THAT?* AND AFTER ALL WE WENT THROUGH GETTIN' IT...JEEZUM CROW!
I BE SPIKE.

HIK UH HHH... EETT...
GODDA FIN'A ***PRIDDY*** ONE.
BE SBIGGE... HIII-KK UH HEE... EET...
ISN'T THAT YOUR SISTER?
HHI-IIK UHHEET...

HIII-KK HEE...EET...
BINCIND!
HIKUH HEETT...
HHI-IIKUHEEET... BE SBIIIGE...

SPIDIDOUD! SPIDIDOUD! NO EADIN' ZOMBIE 'SDUFF! SPIDIDOUD!
WHAK! WHAK! WHAK!
WHAT ABOUT *THAT* NOSE?
IS DAT *BWENDA*?
I'D KNOW?
SHE'D DA *CUDEST* GULL IN SCHOOD. I CAN TAGE EVERTHIN' I NEED FROM HEW!
IKKA... EEEET...

GOOD TO HEAR.
IKKA... HEEET...

BE... SPIGE...
YEEEEEEEEEEEEEEEE!
K-RUNCH!

YEEEE!
SIGH...
KRUNCH! KRUNCH!
YEEEE!

OW... OW... STITCH!
OW...
FIGURE... HF...YOU COULD... HFFA... MAKE *MORE* NOISE?
WE...PF... LOSE HIM?
HELLO?
RAAAHHRRGGH!!

COME UP WITH A PLAN YET?

I'M STICKING WITH "DON'T LET HIM CATCH US".

RRRAAHHRRGH!!

GOOD PLAN.

GOTCHA NOW! GOTCHA GOOD!

HELLO? HEAVY HERE?!
DON'T YOU HATE IT WHEN THEY GET CHATTY?
GONNA MAKE IT LAST! GONNA KILL YOU BOYS BY INCHES FER WHAT YOU DONE T' MY POOR, SWEET CLEO!
HNK... UK...
UGH... WHUG...
YOU BOYS BE DEAD'N' THEN SOME... BETCHA!
CHUNGK!
!!
CHACKT!
NO!

NOOOOOO!
SPLOOT!
FIGURE HE'S DOWN FOR GOOD?
THERE'S A BIT OF LUCK.

ASK THEM.
GOOD POINT.
P.B.W

SO?
SO WHAT?
SO WHAT DO WE DO ABOUT HIM?

HIKKIH...HEE-EEK...
BE SBIGGE...
Hardware
HIKKUH HEEK...

HIKUH...HEEEK...
...HEEEK... BE SBIGGE...
WE ARM OURSELVES.
Hardware
HIK...KUH HEEK...

SH-SH!
IS THE SURPRISE ATTACK! MAKES THE BIG SURPRISE AND SPANKS HIS BROWN BOTTOM BACK TO THE POO PLACE FOREVER AND EVERS!
NO...REALLY. I'M GONNA BE SICK...
SURPRISE...?
IS THE BIG SURPRISE! YAY!

UNCLEAN!
UNCLEAN!
CUTS OUT THE POOTIE PARTS!
CHOKKA-CHOKKA-CHOKKA-CHOKKA...
OUT! OUT, CHONKLIT MONKEYS!
IS THE POWER OF CHRIST COMPELS YOU!
HK...
CHOKKA-CHOKKA-
CHOKKA-CHOKKA...
CHOPS THE POOTIE PARTS!
CHOPS OUT THE CHONKLIT MONKEYS!
CHOKKA-CHOKKA-
HR-GRGLE-GRKL-GNK!
CHOKKA-CHOKKA...
HA! IS THE BIG SURPRISE!
CHOPS YOU OUT!
CHOKKA-CHOKKA-CHOKKA-
KAK! KAK-AK! COUGH!
CHOKKA...
CHOPS OUT THE CHONKLIT MONKEYS!
CLEANSES THE POOTIE PARTS WE DOES!
CHOKKA-CHOKKA-CHOKKA-CHOKKA-
CHOK!
IS TIME FOR SPANKING THE BROWN BOTTOM! YAY!
YEEK!

IS NOW TO MAKE THE SPANKINGS OF THE BROWN BOTTOM! SENDS VIVIAN, KING OF THE CHONKLIT MONKEYS BACK TO THE POO PLACE AND MAKES IT SAFE FOR TRICK OR TREATER TIME! *YAY!*
EUW... EUW... EUW...

MAKES THE SPANKINGS! YAY!

MAKES THE SPANK-INGS...

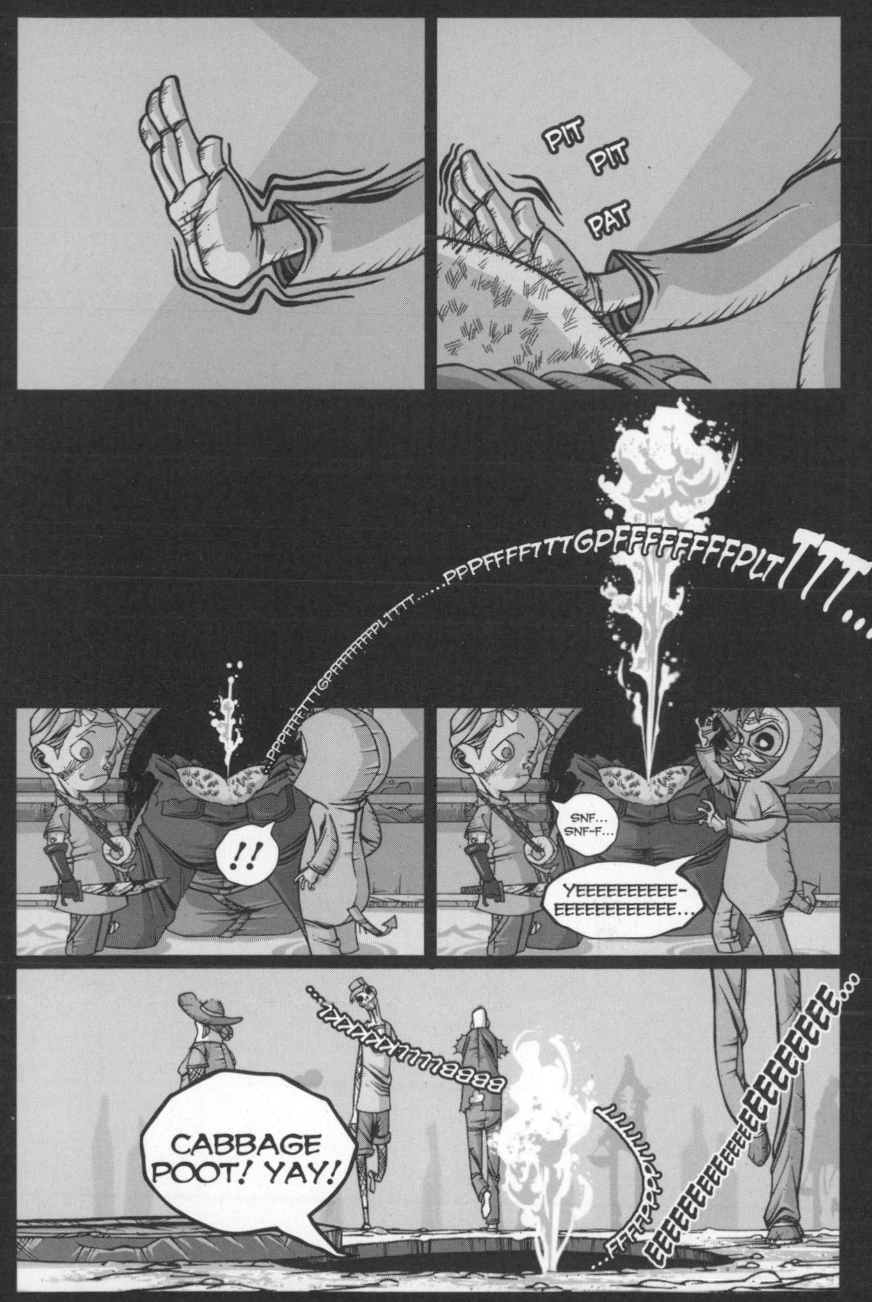
PIT
PIT
PAT
...PPPFFFFFTTTGPFFFFFFFFFPLTTTT.....PPPFFFFTTTGPFFFFFFFFFFPLTTTT...
!!
SNF... SNF-F...
YEEEEEEEEEE-EEEEEEEEEEE...
CABBAGE POOT! YAY!

Cade's Hardware
Propane refill.
Ask for assistance
...SURE YOU WANNA BE WHACKING IT LIKE THAT? I MEAN, ONE SPARK AND...
TANG! TANG! TANG! TANG!
CAUTION FLAMMABLE
NO TRESPASSING
NO. REALLY. MY DAD'S GRILL? ONE MATCH AND IT'S UP AND RUNNING.
I BE SPIKE.
TOL'JA I HEARD BANGING.
!!
TANG! TANG! TANG! TANG!
I SAY WE WASTE 'EM.
ISN'T THAT YOUR BROTHER?
WHY? YOU WANT DIBS ON HIM?
TANG! TANG! TANG! TANG!

HEY!
HOW MANY TIMES I GOTTA TELL YOU NOT TO HANG OUT WITH SPAZMOS?
YOU'RE THE EPILEPTIC KID, RIGHT?
I AIN'T NO SPAZMO!
TANG! TANG! TANG! TANG!
HE'S TRYING TO MAKE A BOMB. SOME LADY RENEGED.
WHY IS HE TRYING TO BLOW US ALL UP?
TANG! TANG! TANG! TANG!
RENEGED...
Y'KNOW. NO TREAT SO YOU GOTTA TRICK.
WITH A BOMB.
AND THIS WORKS FOR YOU?
TANG! TANG! TANG! TANG!
I DON'T CARE SO LONG'S SOME OF THEM UNDEAD THINGS PAY FOR SPEWING ALL OVER MY CANDY.
TANG! TANG! TANG! TANG!
TANG!
TANG!
TANG!
TANG!

COUNT US IN.
IS THE MUCH BIG, OOMPAH OOMPAH VICTORY PARADE! SPANKED HIS BROWN BOTTOM WE DID!
BAWWWWW... SNF... BAWWWWW-AWWW...
IS TRICK OR TREATERS FOR EVERYONE! YAY!
HIKUH HEETT...
HIII-KK UH HEE... EET...
HHI-IIKUHEEET... BE SBIIIGE...

HIII...KUH HEET...
BE SBIGE... HIII-KK UH HEEEET...
HHI-IIK UHEEET...
CHUNK!
CHUNK!
OW!
HOLD STILL!
OWW!! OW!
NO PAIN, NO GAIN.
HOW CUM DEY NEBBER BIDE ON YOU?
GUESS THEY DON'T LIKE SPICY FOOD. DON'T MOVE.
ID HURDS! IT WEAWY, WEAWY HURDS!
CHUNK!
OW! OW! OW!
ALMOST DONE.

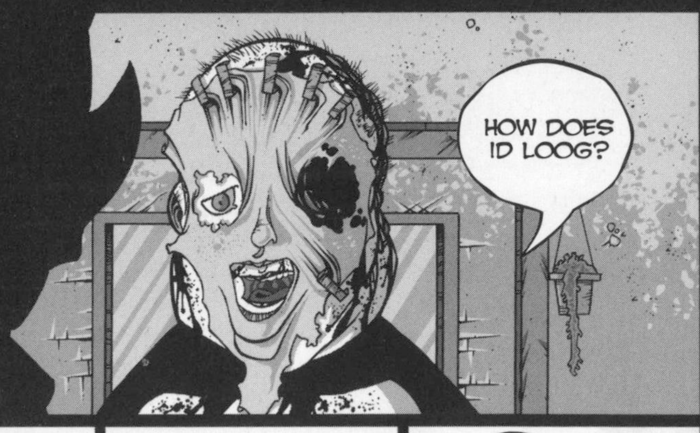
HOW DOES ID LOOG?

IS THIS WHERE I LIE TO YOU?

BAWWWWWWWWWWWW!
I'M *HIDEOD!* DEY ADE ME UGWY!
BAWWWWWWWWWWWW!
A-HUH... SNF... A-HUH...
SNFFL... UH HUH...
'BOUT DONE?

CHUNK!
OW!
SSHHH-GLKGHH...
SHU'UB, BINCEND! DIS IS AW YER FAWD! YUH NOD DUPPOSE D' EAD YER SISDER! WAID'LL I DELL MOM!
GLK?
SHU' UB!!
MAYBE SUMMAGEUB? LIGE MAZGARRA OR LIBSDIK?
SURE. THAT'LL WORK. HOLD STILL...
CHUNK!
OW!
OW!! YOU'W ENJOYN' DIS!
WELL, D'UH!
CHUNK! CHUNK!
HIK UH HHH... EETT...
BE SBIGGE... HIII-KK UH HEE...EET...
MMMAAAAAACKG... 'CLOOOODED...
HHI-IIK UHHEET...

I LUV HALLOWEEN™

CHAPTER SIX: YAY!

MAAAA-GK... 'CLOOOOODED...
HIKUH HEETT... BE SBIGGE...
...HIII-KK UH HEE...EET...
HHI-IIK UHHEET... 'CLOOOODED...
IS THE VICTORY LAP, OOMPAH OOMPAH, YAY! MAKES THE CROWD GO WILD!
SNF... SNFL...
...MAGCK?
I WANNA GO HOME...
SNF... WANNA GO HOME...
HELLO PIGGY BOY. IS THE DING DONG IS DEAD PARADE! YAY!
IS SAFE AGAIN FOR THE TRICK OR TREATINGS!
PIG PIG?

!!

HHHIKKUH... HE-EEET...

SPLUT!
EUW! EUW! EUW! EUW! EUW!
VEWA?

I'D ME...
YEEEeeeeeeeeeeeeeeeeeeeeeeeEE!

YEEeeeeeeeeeeeeeeeeeeeeeeeeeeeEE!
...BIBIAN?

YEEEEEEEEEEEEEEEEEEEEEEEEEEEEEEEEEEE!

YOU CAN HARDLY BLAME HER. YOU ARE HIDEOUS.
WAIT FOR IT...
BAWWWWWWWWWWWWWWW!
!
!
HIKKUH...HEET?
BAWWWWWWWWWWWWWWWWWW!
I'B UGWY! DEY ADE ME UGWY!
BAWWWWWWWWWWWWWWWWWW!
HIIKUH HEET-TT...
BE SBIGE... HIII-KK UH HEET...
HHI-IIK...UHEEET...
'CLOOODED... HIKKUH HEET...
NOW I'B NEBBER BE BOBULAR! NOBUDY WIKES D' UGWY GUHL...
HEY!
HEY!
GID AWAY FUM... DON' TOUDCH ME! BAD! BAD DOMBIES! GED AWAY!
HIIKUH HEETT... 'CLOOODED...
HHI-IIK... UHEEET... BE SBIGE...
HIII-KK UH HEET...
HIIIIKKUH HEET...

BE SBIGE... IIKUH HEET...
HIIKK UH HEET...
SHRIK-KK!
YEEK!
SCREECH!
RIP!
POP!
I DUNNO. SEEM PRETTY POPULAR TO ME.
HHI-IIK... HEEET... BE SBIGE...
HIIIIKKUH HEET... 'CLOO- OOODED...

SURE YOU KNOW WHICH ONE IT IS? THERE'S A LOT OF PIPES 'N' LIKE DOWN THERE.
HEY! EASY!
I BE SPIKE.
Hardware
YOU BE DEAD YOU DROP THIS ON MY FOOT AGAIN!
IT'S ALWAYS THE ONE WITH THE BIG RED VALVE IN THE MOVIES. LOOK FOR A BIG RED VALVE.
HOW 'BOUT ONE SAYS "GAS MAIN"?
THAT'S GOOD. THAT'S THE ONE.
SIGH...
Turgid Meadows
PSG&E GAS MAIN
EXERCISE EXTREME CAUTION

GOT THE THIRD ONE?

I BE SPIKE.

Turgid Meadows
PSG&E GAS MAIN
EXERCISE EXTREME CAUTION

SEND IT DOWN AND DOUSE THE FUSE.

INCOMING!

CLANK!

CLUNG-GG!

THUDUP!

HEH...

ASSHOLE.

I STILL DON'T GET IT.

THAT'S 'CAUSE YOU'RE A SPAZMO.
I AIN'T NO SPAZMO!
LOOK AROUND, SPAZMO. THEY ROBBED US OF OUR HALLOWEEN. HIJACKED THE WHOLE NIGHT!
NOW WE GET US SOME PAYBACK.
THAT'S NOT WHAT I...I'M ALL FOR TAKING THEM DOWN. SPLOOCHED ALL OVER MY CANDY! YOU SHOULD'A SEEN THE SIZE'A THE BAG!
YEH... HEH... HOOOO...
IT WAS...
WHAT I DON'T GET'S WHY WE GOTTA USE THE PROPANE. WHY NOT JUST OPEN THE GAS MAIN AND TOSS A MATCH?
BECAUSE THEN WE GET BLOWN UP TOO.
THE FUSE?!

...BE SURE THE PROPANE'LL BLOW THE MAIN?
Cade's Hardware
Propane refill.
Ask for assistance
A BOMB'S A BOMB. GOT *THREE* DOWN THERE.
CAUTION FLAMMABLE
SSSSSSSSSSSSSSSSSSSSSSSSSSSSSSSSSSSSS...
YEAH... YEAH. THREE *OUGHTA* DO IT...
WON'T KNOW TIL IT'S DONE.
HOW LONG YOU FIGURE?
LONG ENOUGH TO GIVE US A GOOD HEAD START.
HOW LONG'S THAT?
SSSSSSSSSSSSSSSSS...
LOOK... *REALLY...* YOU GOT TO STOP TALKING. *NOW*. JUST... *STOP*.
SSSSSSSSSSSSSSSSSSSSSS...

SSSSSSSSSSSSSSSSSS...
SSSSSSSSSSSSSSSSSS...
SSSSSSSSSSSSSSSSSS...
WHY'S THAT? WHY I GOTTA STOP TALKING? YOU GOTTA, LIKE, CONCENTRATE?
SSSSSSSSSSSSSSSS...
HAND ME THOSE, WOULD'JA?

IIKUH HEET...
HIIKK UH HEET...
BE SBIGE...
...!
HIIIIKKUH HEET... 'CLOO-OOODED...
SPIKE. WHAT'S THE GOOD WORD?
I BE SPIKE.
DEVIL LAD?
FINCH?
WHERE YOU BEEN ALL NIGHT?
I COULD ASK YOU THE SAME.
SO... WHAT'S WITH THE SEWER?
WE'RE GONNA BLOW UP THE TOWN.
BECAUSE?
"HIIKUH HEET."

HIKUH... HEEET...
HIK-KKUH HEEEET... BE SBIGE...
RIGHT.
Hardware
NO. I BE SPIKE.
PROPANE BOMB.
HOW?
BLOW THE GAS MAIN?
UH HUH.
COOL.
EVER SEE ONE OF THESE UP CLOSE?
THAT SOMEONE'S TONGUE?
THAT *KITTY*? ...YOU GOT THE FUSE?
NO MOSS GROWING ON *YOU*.
HI-IIKUH HEET... BE SBIGE...
JERK IT FROM ONE'A THEM?
NO. *I* BE SPIKE.
BE SBIGE...
NO. *I* BE SPIKE.

KINDA...
Cade's Hardware
Propane refill.
Ask for assistance
CAUTION
FLAMMABLE
B-B-B-B-G-
G-G-G-B-B-
G-G-B-B-G-
G...
NO
TRESPASSING

HIKUH HEET...
YAY!
BE SBIGE...
HIKUH HEEET...
HHHIK..UHHHET...
BE SBIGE...
...'CLOOOOD-
ED... BE SBIGE.
HIKUH... HEET...
HIKUH HEEET...
SPLUKT!
BE SBIGE...
HHHIK..UHHHET...
MMMA-
AAAGK...

RAWNCH!
PLAY NICE.

HIKIUH HEEET... BE SBIGE...
HI-IIIKUH HEE-EET...
...'CLOOODED...
GASP... *VINCENT!*
!!
WELL TONIGHT HAS BEEN A TOTAL *BUST*.
TELL ME. CAN YOU BELIEVE HE UP AND GOT HIMSELF KILLED?
YEAH. WE'RE GOING TO HAVE TO RETHINK THIS WHOLE "ROYAL LINEAGE" THING.

LEWIS THINKS A PARLIAMENTARY STRUCTURE ISN'T OUT OF THE QUESTION.
LEWIS IS A MORON. YOU KNOW HOW HARD IT IS TO GET A CONSENSUS VOTE WHEN THE REPRESENTATIVES ARE FLINGING POOP AT ONE ANOTHER?
I CAN'T BELIEVE HE GOT HIMSELF *KILLED!*
WHAT ARE WE GOING TO DO WITH ALL OF THESE PIES?
SURE BET THE FAIR'S BEEN CANCELED... DAMN! I LEFT MY DURAN DURAN CD IN THERE.
RELAX. IT'S NOT GOING ANYWH...
YEEEEEEEEEEEEEEEEEEEEEEEEE!
EEEEEEEEEEEEEEEEEEEEEEEEEE
NOW WHAT WAS *THAT* ALL ABOUT?

BE SBIGE...
NO. BAD ZOMBIES! I BE SPIKE!
HHHI-II BE SBIGE...
SSSSSSSSSSSSSSSSSSSSSS...
Turgid Meadows PSG&E GAS MAIN
EXERCISE EXTREME CAUTION
NO! I BE SPIKE!
HIKKUH... HEEET...
NO! I BE SPIKE!
BE SBIGE...
NO! I BE SPIKE!
...'CLOO-OOOODED...
BE SBIGE...
NO! I BE SPIKE!
HIKUH HEEET... BE SBIGE...
BE SBIGE...
NO! I BE SPIKE!

WELL...
NO TIME LIKE THE PRESENT.
UH UH.
LIGHT IT AND RUN LIKE HELL.
YOU SURE WE CAN'T CRASH WITH YOU TIL WE FIND...
UH HUH.
WE'LL MANAGE.
YOU HAVE NO IDEA WHAT A BAD IDEA THAT IS.
HERE GOES. GET READY.

FSK!
BWOOOOOOSSSSSHHHH!
THAT CAN'T BE GOOD.
HOW MUCH PROPANE'D YOU USE?
UM... TOO MUCH?

WHUMP-
UMP-
UMP-
UMP-
WHABOO

OOOOMM!
WELCOME
TO
TURGID MEADOW

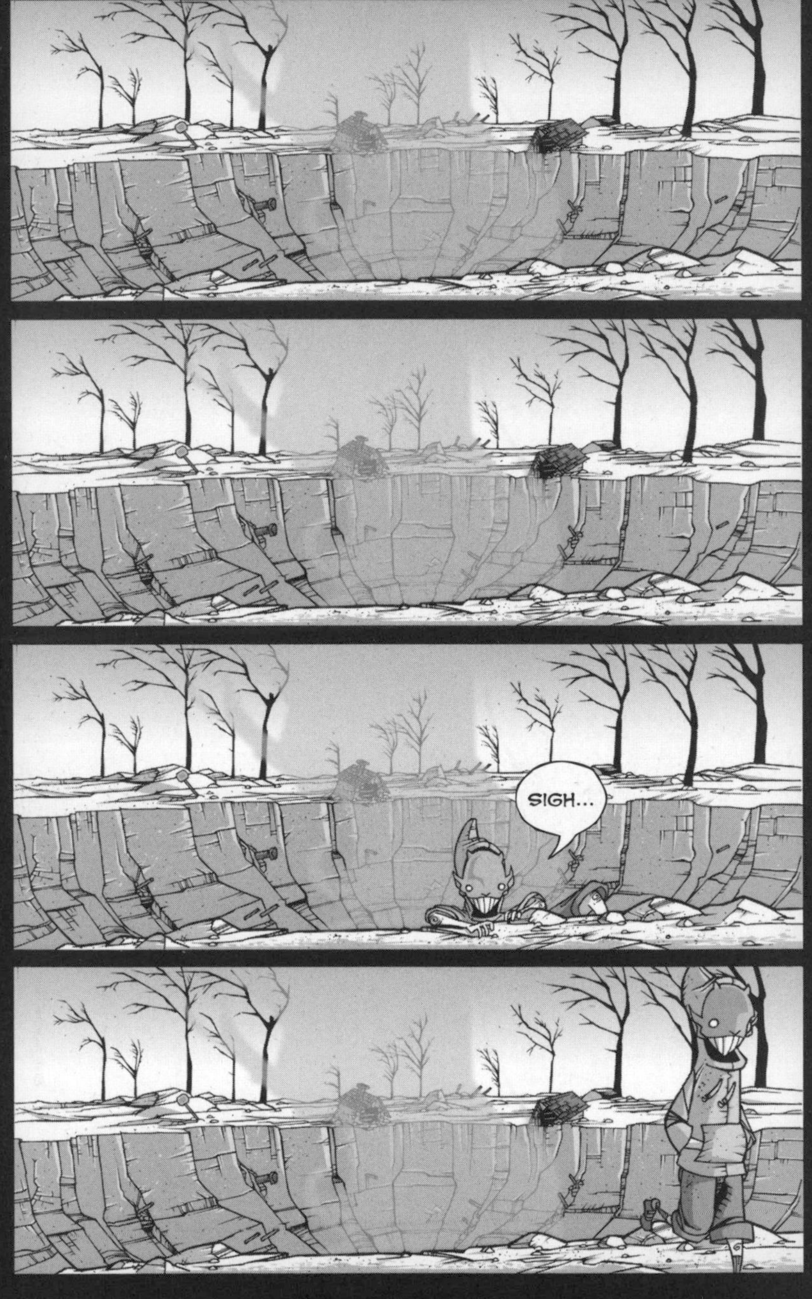
SIGH...

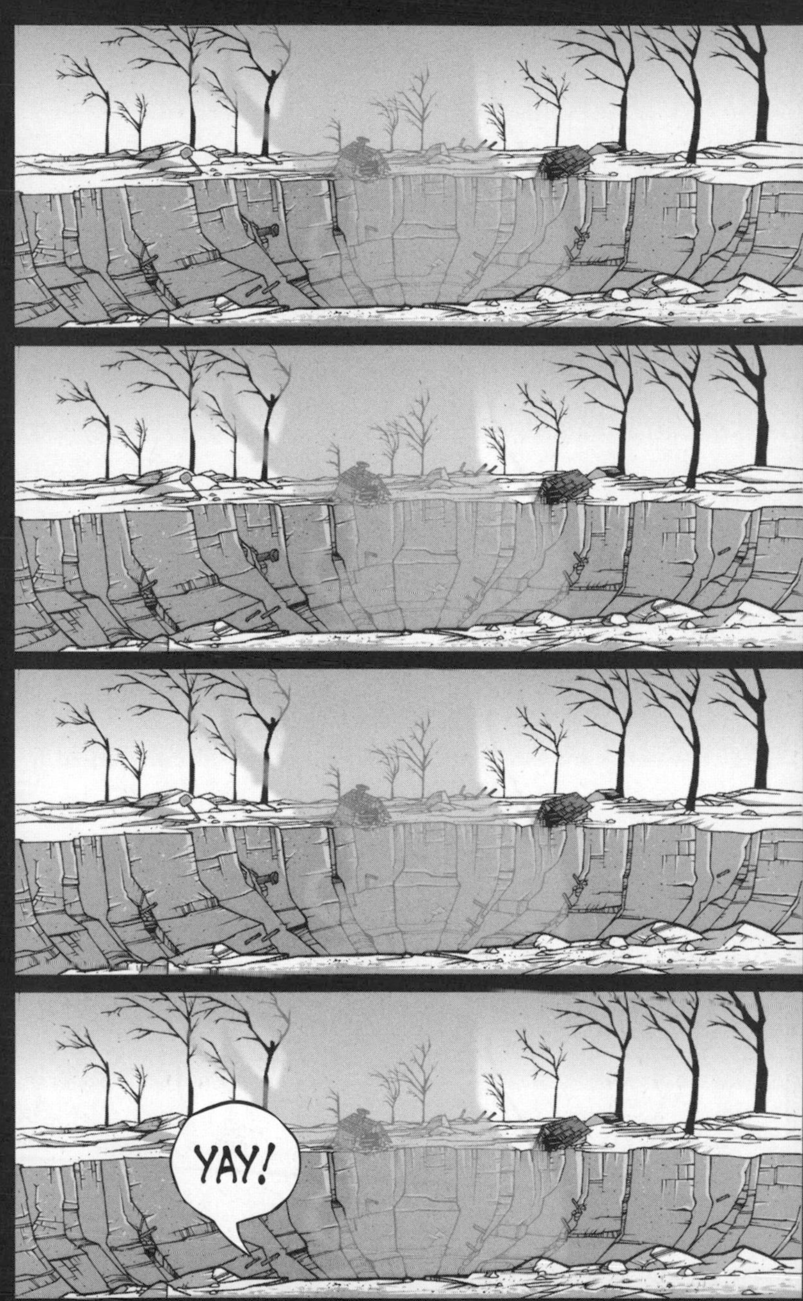
YAY!

THE THIRD BOOK TAKES PLACE DURING AN ABORTIVE *INVASION ATTEMPT* BY ALIENS WHO LOOK TOO MEXICAN TO BE TAKEN SERIOUSLY. NO, I'M NOT KIDDING.

NEW CHARACTERS ARE KEVIN KYLE KRAMER (FINCH'S AGE), A.K.A *TRIPLE K*. HE'S THE BLACK KID.

AND ***MONICA*** (13) WHO KILLS DOGS.

-KEITH GIFFEN

(TAKEN FROM AN EMAIL SENT TO THE EDITOR)

i Luv Halloween
SKETCHBOOK

Me am Zombie moochie!

I LUV HALLOWEEN
SKETCHBOOK

Perfect
Puzzled look.
always has
a stupid lo

feels
empty, keep
Goggles always
on top.

Vera
mask off

I LUV HALLOWEEN SKETCHBOOK

I LUV HALLOWEEN
SKETCHBOOK

I LUV HALLOWEEN SKETCHBOOK

I LUV HALLOWEEN
SKETCHBOOK

Zombie
Finch!

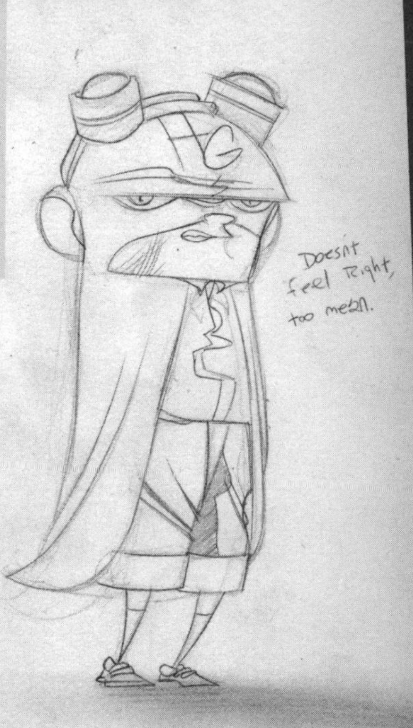
Doesn't
feel Right,
too mean.

Sisters
ROMAN.05
"I LuV HaLLoween"

Creator Bios

Benjamin Roman

Keith Giffen is a veteran comic book writer and is probably best known for his critically acclaimed work on the titles Justice League and Legion of Super-Heroes. He currently does the English language adaptations of Battle Royale and Battle Vixens for Tokyopop.

Benjamin Roman was raised in Miami, where he worked and worked and worked on his portfolio, preparing it for con season. For 5 or 6 years, he went to San Diego and Chicago to try to get an editor, any editor, to look at it. After minimal success with one or two publishers, Roman had just about given up on trying to break into the industry, so he decided to move to Los Angeles. He got a job at a copy shop in Hollywood and assimilated into the strange and remarkable world that is L.A. One day a guy walked in and placed an order. After a brief conversation, Roman told the guy that he was an illustrator and proceeded to show him some art samples. After a few months went by, the guy returned to tell Benjamin Roman that he showed the samples to his editor and that his editor wanted to discuss publishing "I Luv Halloween" as a full-length series. The rest, as they say, is history. Go figure.

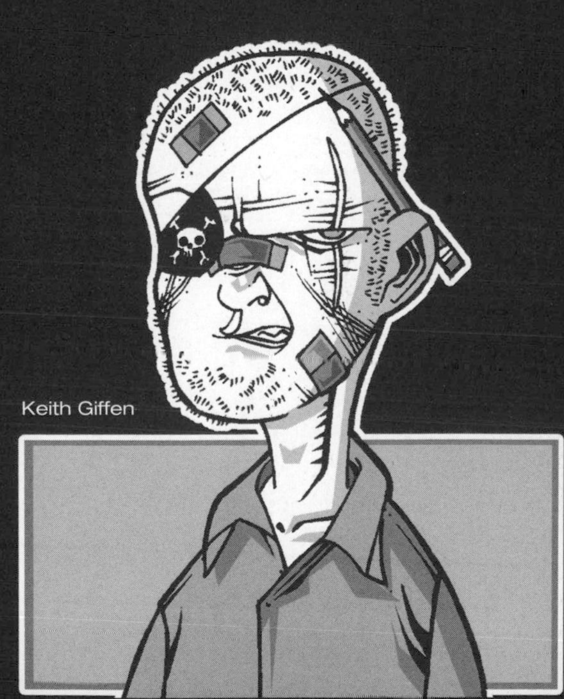

Keith Giffen

Hans Steinbach's

A MIDNIGHT OPERA

For nearly a millennium, undead creatures have blended into a Europe driven by religious dogma... Ein DeLaLune is an underground Goth metal sensation on the Paris music scene, tragic and beautiful. He has the edge on other Goth music powerhouses...he's undead, a fact he's kept hidden for centuries. But his newfound fame might just bring out the very phantoms of his past from whom he has been hiding for centuries, including his powerful brother, Leroux. And if the two don't reconcile, the entire undead nation could rise up from the depths of modern society to lay waste to mankind.

Reunited under the direst of circumstances, the undead brothers Ein and Leroux DeLaLune rush to get the rest of the immortals out of Paris and away from the pagan magic of the witch Elizabeth Bathory. However, the witch is having doubts about her poisonous role in the peaceful existence the brothers have built for the undead over the past 400 years, which could cause a rift between her and Victor Frankenstein, who is carrying out her plan with fervor. The key to saving the undead citizens may rest in the human Dahlia Whyte, who is still reeling from learning that her lover Ein is actually a dark creature of the night.

Paris
Five years ago...
WE AIN'T GETTIN' IN THERE. IT'S A BUNCH O'FANCY PANTS.
COME ON, SLAGS. ONE OF US CAN SWEET TALK THE TOSSER AT THE DOOR.
YEAH, ALL RIGHT. I'LL DO IT.

VIRTUOSO
HELLO, HANDSOME. LITTLE ME AND MY FRIENDS O'PLENTY ARE ALL DOLLED UP WITH NO WHERE TO GO.
...
HOW HARD CAN PULLIN' A FROG BE?

WE'RE ONLY IN FOR THE NIGHT AND WOULD DO **ANYTHING** TO GET A GANDER AT THIS CHIC PARISIAN CLUB SCENE WE'VE HEARD SO MUCH ABOUT.
OUI?
OUI.
OUI.
OR MAYBE YOU DON'T WANT THE GRATITUDE OF A FINE BRITISH LASS.
FRENCH MEN ARE ALL POOF-TERS.
THAT COY POUT WAS CUTE.
AH, DHALIA, DAHLING. YA DIDN'T EVEN PUT A DENT IN 'IM.

GOTTA MAKE A CALL, LOVES.
JEAN PAUL?
SO I GOT IN EASY, YOU CYNICAL MAN. BUT YOU'RE RIGHT, IT'S JUST A HAVEN FOR FEATHER-DUSTED LOUCES.
WHERE'S YOUR PARTY?

AT-VANCE
METAL
GAMMA RAY
POWER METAL
tonight:
Einblick
DELALUNE
NEO-CLASSICAL
MADNESS!!!

Einblick
DELALUNE
IRON SAVIOR
MAXIMUM POWER!!
TURN AROUND!
YOU SUCK!
What? He thinks he's Jim Morrison?
WHO THE HELL IS THIS SON OF A BITCH?
GET OFF THE STAGE!

pwoooohhh

AAGGGHHHHHHHHHHHHH

twirl

clap
ROCK ON!
AHHHH!
WHOOOOO!
I LOVE YOU!

ROADSONG

Music...mystery...and Murder!

ROADSONG

Monty and Simon form the ultimate band on the run when they go on the lam to the seedy world of dive bars and broken-down dreams in the Midwest. There Monty and Simon must survive a walk on the wild side while trying to clear their names of a crime they did not commit! Will music save their mortal souls?

READ A CHAPTER OF THE MANGA ONLINE FOR FREE:

WWW.TOKYOPOP.COM/ROADSONG